TWO SUNS RISING

TWO SUNS RISING

A
COLLECTION
OF
SACRED
WRITINGS

—

JONATHAN
STAR

CASTLE BOOKS
Edison, New Jersey

This edition published in 1996 by
CASTLE BOOKS
A Division of Book Sales, Inc.
114 Northfield Avenue, Edison, New Jersey 08837

Published by arrangement with Bantam Books.

ISBN 0-7858-0723-3

Library of Congress Cataloging-in-Publication Data

Star, Jonathan.
   Two suns rising : a collection of sacred writings / Jonathan Star.
      p.   cm.
   Includes bibliographical references (p. 245)
   ISBN 0-7858-0723-3
   1. Sacred books.   2. Religious literature, English.   I. Title.
BL7Q.S73   1991
291.8—dc29   90-21642
                                                        CIP

MANUFACTURED IN THE UNITED STATES OF AMERICA.

CONTENTS

SAGES OF TAOISM

BUDDHIST MASTERS

WISDOM OF THE HEBREWS

STOIC PHILOSOPHERS

SUFI POETS

CHRISTIAN SAINTS

POET-SAINTS OF INDIA

To
Baba,
Gurumayi,
and the most precious thing in this world—
the love in a human heart.

What a day today.
There are two Suns rising!
What a day,
Not like any other day.
Look!
The Light is shining in your heart,
The wheel of life has stopped.
Oh, you who can see into your own heart,
What a day,
This is your day.

—*Rumi*

FOREWORD

In every civilization throughout history, there have been great beings who have made the same supreme discovery—that the God they sought for so many years was no different than their own selves. Each generation is blessed by these enlightened souls who spread only goodness throughout the world and have the power to grant a divine boon—the boon of perfect wisdom. "When the mysterious Unity between the soul and the Divine becomes clear," wrote the Sufi master Ibn al Arabi, "you will realize that you are none other than God. You will see all your actions as His actions; all your features as His features; all your breaths as His breath." This is the vision of a perfect being; this is the vision they impart to others.

Each tradition honors these great teachers, these "kings among men" who lead people back to their own perfection. The Taoists call them *Sheng Jen*, "those who hear the voice of the Absolute"; the Hindus call them *Siddhas*, "perfect"; to the Buddhists they're *Buddhas,* "the awakened ones"; to the Sufis, *Pir,* "Master"; and to the Christians, they're called *Saints.*

The poems, teachings, and stories in this collection are written by these "perfect beings"; and their every word has the power to bring us into their world, to put us in their company, and to coax us inward with the irresistible invitation to experience our own truth. Through their words we sense the wonder of a magical place within us—a world of pulsating consciousness, of sheer delight, of unbounded love, of supreme beauty; a world where all the universe is united in a grand fellowship of bliss. So come, let us enter this world, and let the words of these noble souls lead us to the greatness and joy that lies within our own hearts.

Scriptures of India

—

RIG VEDA
UPANISHADS
BHAGAVAD GITA
GURU GITA
VISHNU SAHASRANAM

अरुण उत बभ्रुः सुमङ्गलः
श्रिताः सहस्रशोवैषाꣲ हेळ
र्पति नीलग्रीवो विलोहित
ह्हायैं। उतैनं विश्वा भूतार्ा
र्मों अस्तु नीलग्रीवाय सह
त्वानोऽहं तेभ्योऽकरं न
गुभयोरार्लिंयोऽज्याम्। याश्व
प॥   ॥ अवतल्य ध
नेशीर्य शल्यानां मुखा शि
वेज्यं धनुः कपर्दिनो विश
येषव आभुरस्य निषङ्गथिः॥
भूव ते धनुः। तयास्मा
  ॥ नमस्ते अस्त्वायुधा
त ते नमो बाहुभ्यां तब ध
तिरसान्वृणक्तु विभतः।

The scriptures that form the foundation of the Hindu religion are considered direct revelations of the Truth from God. In China, scriptures are often attributed to some great personage, as a way to give them authenticity, but in India, God is considered the author, and the sages who actually penned the words are of little importance.

The *Vedas,* which means "knowledge" or "sacred teachings," are a vast collection of Sanskrit hymns, prayers, and ritual instruction, composed between the fifteenth and tenth centuries B.C. These works are divided into four books. The first of these—and the oldest scripture of India—is called the **Rig Veda,** a group of hymns praising the gods, the elements, and the bounty of the earth. At the end of each Veda is a section called the **Upanishads,** which means "sitting close with devotion." These contain the "secret teachings" of the ancients, which, over the centuries, have been well guarded, and meant only for the most worthy disciples. The *Upanishads* inquire into the nature of reality, God, and the universe; they are more probing and inquisitive than the rest of the Vedas, focusing on how to experience God directly. The *Upanishads* state that the Absolute Reality, *Brahman,* dwells fully in the human spirit; and that this Reality can be known and is meant to be known. The teachings found in the *Upanishads* are often referred to as *Vedanta,* meaning "at the end of the Vedas."

Another treasure of Indian spirituality, originating between the 5th and 2nd centuries B.C., is the *Mahabharata,* a great epic filled with popular myth, legends, spiritual lessons, and historical accounts of the war between two sides of the noble Bharata family. Within this sweeping poetic drama is found the **Bhagavad Gita** ("The Song of God"), which is among the most famous and revered dialogues in all of religious literature. The *Bhagavad Gita* opens when the final battle is about to begin: the famed archer Arjuna and his charioteer, Lord Krishna, ride out between the two opposing armies. When Arjuna sees his teachers and cousins on one side and his brothers on the other, he becomes utterly dejected and doubtful about his duty as a warrior. Krishna instructs Arjuna about duty, knowledge, the path of union with God (*yoga*) and the secret of non-action. Krishna then reveals his true identity as the Supreme Lord and gives Arjuna a vision of his all-pervasive form. Inspired, Arjuna regains his vigor and is ready to fight. The sage Sanjaya narrates the whole story to the blind king Dhritarashtra from a nearby hill.

Within the *Mahabharata* is another well-known section called the **Vishnu Sahasranam** ("The Thousand Names of God"), a compendium of a thousand different aspects, powers, names, and forms of the Supreme Lord.

According to long tradition, spiritual realization comes only through the grace of a Guru, or spiritual Master; and many Indian scriptures take the form of this essential dialogue between Guru and disciple. The **Guru Gita** (?6th century A.D.) is one such text, a garland of rhythmic verses in which Lord Shiva, the Primordial Guru, tells his wife, Parvati, about the Guru–disciple relationship; the need for devotion to the Guru; and the secret knowledge that the Guru is none other than *Brahman*. Of this text, the twentieth-century Indian Saint Swami Muktananda said, "If anyone were to ask me which is the one indispensable text, I would answer, 'the *Guru Gita*.' This is so supremely holy that it makes the ignorant learned, the utterly poor wealthy, and the scholarly fully realized."

Rig Veda

HYMN OF CREATION

In the beginning
There was neither existence nor nonexistence,
Neither sky nor heaven beyond . . .

That One breathed, without breath, by its own power,
Nothing else was there . . .

The first born was the Creative Will,
The primordial seed of the mind.
The sages, searching for the truth within their own hearts,
Realized the eternal bond between the seen and
    the unseen.

This bond was an endless line stretched across the heavens.
What was above?
What was below?
Primal seeds were sprouting, mighty forces moving,
Pulsation below, pure energy above.

Who here knows? Who can say for sure?
When it began and from where it came—this creation?
The gods came afterwards,
So who really knows?

From where this creation came,
Whether He formed it or not,
He who watches everything from the highest heaven,
Only He knows—or perhaps even He does not know!

Upanishads

Though the Infinite One is without color,
He colors the entire universe;
Though immortal,
He is born, lives, and dies.
That One is all that was, is, and will be
Yet He is always the same.

He is the Supreme, Unchanging Absolute.

He becomes the fire, the sun,
The wind, the moon;
He becomes the starry heavens,
The vast waters, giving life to all.

He becomes the woman, the man,
The youth and the maiden too;
He becomes the old fellow
Tottering on his staff;
He becomes every face
Looking in every direction.

He becomes the blue butterfly,
The green parrot with red eyes;
He becomes lightning, the seasons,
The endless seas.

Without birth or death,
Beyond all time and space,
He is the One from whom
Every world is born.

Upanishads

There once lived a boy named Svetaketu. At the age of twelve his father said to him, "Son, go find a teacher and learn the sacred wisdom of the Vedas which everyone in our family knows." So Svetaketu went off. Twelve years later he returned—versed in all the Vedas, skilled in all the arts, proficient in all the sciences, and quite arrogant. His father said to him,

"Svetaketu, I see your knowledge is so great."

"Yes it is, sir."

"You have mastered the most abstruse teachings."

"Yes, I have, sir."

"So tell me, have you ever asked for that knowledge whereby you can hear what cannot be heard, see what cannot be seen, and know what cannot be known?"

"What knowledge is that, sir?"

"By knowing one lump of clay, you know all that is made of clay; by knowing one nugget of gold, you know all that is made of gold; so, by knowing that one principle which fills the universe, you know all the universe."

"What principle is that, sir?"

"It is the principle of pure existence. It is the essence of that one Primal Being, who, at the very beginning, formed the universe, filled it with himself, and entered into every creature. That One alone is the essence of all, the soul of the world, the eternal truth, the Supreme Self; and, O Svetaketu, you are That!"

"Please sir, instruct me further."

"So be it, my son. Look at these rivers: some flow toward the east, others toward the west, but all come from the sea and all return to the sea. When they're surging rivers they know not where they come from, and when they merge into the sea they no longer think, "I am this river, I am that river." In the same way, all creatures in this world—a tiger, a lion, a bear, a wolf, a worm, a gnat, or a mosquito—have come from Pure Being yet do not know it. That one alone is the essence of all, the soul of the world, the eternal truth, the Supreme Self; and, O Svetaketu, you are That!"

"Please sir, instruct me further."

"So be it, my son. Bring me a fruit from that Nyagroda tree." Svetaketu picked a fruit and brought it to his father:

"Here it is, sir."

"Break it open."

"I have broken it, sir."

"What do you see there?"

"Little seeds."

"Break open one of them."

"I have broken it, sir."

"What do you see there?"

"Nothing at all."

"My son, that subtle essence which you cannot see, it is by that very essence that this great Nyagroda tree stands. Believe it my son, that one alone is the essence of all, the soul of the world, the eternal truth, the Supreme Self; and, O Svetaketu, you are That!"

"Please sir, instruct me further."

"So be it, my son. Put this salt in the water and come back tomorrow."

Svetaketu did so and returned the next morning. His father said,

"Please return to me the salt you placed in the water yesterday."

Svetaketu looked but could not find it:

"But sir, all the salt has dissolved."

"How does the water at the top taste?"

"Like salt."

"And at the middle?"

"Like salt."

"And at the bottom?"

"Like salt."

"My son, the salt remains in the water even though you do not see it; and though you do not see that Pure Being he is fully present in you and everywhere else. That one alone is the essence of all, the soul of the world, the eternal truth, the Supreme Self; and, O Svetaketu, you are That! You are That!"

UPANISHADS

The Lord of all,
   The knower of all,
   The beginning and end of all—
That Self dwells in every human heart.
Look out—it's gone.
Look in—it's gone.
Don't look—it's gone.
It cannot be remembered,
It cannot be forgotten,
It cannot be grasped by any possible means.
It is beyond all limits and bounds.
It is the pure oneness
   where nothing else can exist.

To know it, you must become it!

It is the final resting place of all activity,
   peaceful and unchanging,
   the ultimate good,
   one without a second,
It is the Supreme Self.
It, above all else, should be known.

BHAGAVAD GITA

DIVINE MANIFESTATIONS

Lord Krishna

I am the source of everything,
and all worlds come out of Me;
knowing this, the wise ones honor me
in the cave of their hearts.

To those of unswerving devotion,
who worship me with love,
I give the boon of discrimination
by which they come to me.

Dwelling within
as pure consciousness,
I destroy the darkness born of ignorance
with the shining lamp of true knowledge.

I am the Supreme Self
dwelling in the hearts of all creatures;
they are born in me, sustained by me,
and in the end, return to me.

Listen Arjuna, I can only tell you of
my most prominent forms;
for my divine power
is endless in extent.

Of sun gods, I am Vishnu,
of lights, the radiant sun;

I am chief among the wind gods,
the moon in the starry sky.

Among rituals, I am the chanting of sacred names,
among gods, I am Indra, king of heaven;
among sense organs, I am the mind,
and the pure intelligence of all beings.

I am the glorious Shiva among gods of destruction,
Lord of wealth among the keepers of fortune;
I am the pure flame among the fire gods,
the great Meru among mountain peaks.

O Arjuna, know me as instructor of the gods,
chief of heavenly priests;
of generals I am Skanda, god of war,
of bodies of water, I am the ocean.

Among great sages, I am Brighu,
among words, I am the eternal sound *Om*;
of sacrifices, I am the repetition of God's Name,
of all that is immovable, I am the Himalayas.

Among trees, I am the holy fig tree,
and Narada among divine seers;
of heavenly musicians, I am their leader,
of perfected souls, the sage Kapila.

Of horses, I am the radiant stallion,
born from the ocean of pure nectar;
among royal elephants, I am the king's mount,
among men, their loyal protector.

I am the thunderbolt among weapons,
the wish-fulfilling cow among cattle;
I am the god of love begetting children
and Vasuki, king of the snakes.

I am the endless serpent, Ananta,
the lord of all sea creatures;
I am Aryman, the greatest of the ancestors,
and the Lord of Death, reckoner of every deed.

I am Prahlada, the devoted son of demons,
and Time, the measure of all that endures;
I am the lion among beasts,
and the Lord's eagle among birds.

Of purifiers, I am the wind;
the great Rama among warriors;
I am the shark among sea creatures,
and the River Ganges among all waters that flow.

O Arjuna! Of all creation
I am the beginning, middle, and end;
I am the supreme knowledge of the Self,
the eloquence of every orator.

Of letters, I am the letter *A*,
of compounds, the simple pairing;
I am the Creator facing all directions at once,
and time inexhaustible.

I am Death, devourer of all,
and also the origin of all things yet to be;
among the feminine virtues I am fame, fortune,
eloquence, wisdom, gratitude, patience, and forgiveness.

I am the Great Chant of the ancients,
the metre of Vedic hymns;
the first cool month of the year,
the Spring bursting with flowers.

I am the loaded dice of tricksters,
the radiance of shining heroes;
I am victory, effort,
and the wisdom among the wise.

I am Krishna among the mighty Vrishnis
and Arjuna among the Pandava princes;
I am the great Vyasa among sages,
and Ushana, the illumined poet.

I am the judging rod of rulers,
the shrewd tactics of ambitious men;
I am the silence of secret things,
the truth of ancient knowledge.

O Arjuna, I am the primal seed
of all existence;
no being, moving or unmoving,
can exist without me.

O Great Warrior, there is no end
to the forms of my divine power . . .

All that exists,
all that is beautiful, radiant, and powerful,
is but a spark
of my brilliant Light . . .

And here I stand, supporting the entire world,
with one fragment of my being.

BHAGAVAD GITA

VISION OF GOD'S FORM

Lord Krishna

Arjuna, behold my forms
in the hundreds and thousands;
various, divine,
of every shape and hue.

See the celestial deities, gods of fire,
gods of destruction, twin gods of dawn,
and also gods of thunder; Arjuna,
behold these wonders never seen before.

See now the whole of this universe,
the movable and immovable,
and whatever else you wish to see,
unified, as one, in my body.

But with your own eyes
you cannot see me as I am.
I will give you divine sight.
Now behold the glory of my true form!

Sanjaya

Having thus spoken, O King,
The Great Lord of Yoga
revealed to Arjuna
his supreme form.

It was a wondrous vision of the infinite Lord,
with faces and eyes everywhere;
with celestial ornaments
and heavenly weapons of every kind.

The stream of sights was endless,
revealing every possible marvel:
divine garments and garlands,
the heavens filled with ambrosial perfume.

If the light of a thousand suns
were to blaze in the sky at once,
such would hardly match the splendor
of that Great Being.

Arjuna
I see your infinite form—
arms, bellies, faces, and eyes everywhere;
I see no beginning, middle, or end;
O Lord of the Universe, you are everything!

I see your crown, club, and discus,
your radiant light on all sides;
hard to look at is this blaze of fire and sun
that fills your immeasurable form.

You are the supreme goal of all knowledge,
the ultimate refuge of all the world;
you are the guardian of eternal law,
the innermost spirit of all.

I see your power without beginning, middle, or end;
the sun and moon in your eyes,
the all-consuming fire of your mouth,
the radiance of your light filling the skies.

O Great One, you alone fill
the space between heaven and earth;
seeing your wondrous and awesome form
all the worlds tremble.

I see the hosts of gods entering you,
others, in fear, bow their heads for mercy;
throngs of great seers and perfected beings
praise you with the glorious singing of your Name.

Gods of destruction, gods of light,
celestial beings, angels, heavenly horsemen,
howling wind gods, ancestors,
throngs of heavenly musicians, magical beings,
demons, and those with supernatural powers,
all look at you in wonder.

Seeing your great form,
your countless mouths and eyes,
your numerous arms, legs, feet, bellies,
and terrible fangs, O Krishna,
all the worlds tremble,
and so do I.

O Supreme Lord,
tell me who you are in so frightful a form?

Lord Krishna

I am the all-powerful Time, destroyer of every world,
relentlessly moving all things to their end;
even without you, these warriors,
arrayed in opposing armies, will not survive.

So get up
and win glory!
Conquer your enemies
and enjoy the fullness of your rightful kingdom.
They have already been
slain by me;
O peerless archer, be but
the instrument of my will.

Arjuna

You are the First Being,
the ancient soul of man,
the ultimate resting place of all worlds;
you are the knower, the known,
and the state beyond knowing—
all the universe is filled by you,
O Lord of Infinite Forms.

I thought you were my peer
and rashly called you,
"Krishna," "son of Yadu," "friend";
through negligence, or the blindness of love,
I could not see your greatness.

You are Father of the world,
object of its worship,
most venerable of its masters,
without equal;

who in three worlds could ever
surpass your incomparable might?

Lord Krishna
This vision you have seen
is difficult to obtain;
even the gods are ever wishing
for such a sight.

Not through study of scriptures,
austerities, charity, or sacrifice,
can I be seen
as you have seen me.

O Arjuna, only by the
unswerving love of a human heart,
can my supreme state be seen,
and known, and attained.

Bhagavad Gita

FINAL TEACHING

Lord Krishna

Relying on your own senses,
harboring false compassion,
you think, "I will not fight";
but your resolve is in vain,
your own nature will compel you.

You were born in this world with a duty,
decreed by your own destiny,
what delusion now turns you, Arjuna,
against your own calling?

The Lord of Unlimited Power
dwells in the heart of all beings, Arjuna,
and by His magic power of illusion,
causes them to move about like wooden dolls
fixed on a machine.

Give your whole heart to that Supreme Lord,
seek refuge in Him alone;
by His Grace you will find perfect peace
and the abode of immortal life.

Go deeper and deeper within yourself
until nothing is left—
then act.

No one on earth is more dear to me than you;
that is why I tell you all this . . .

Abandon all hope of gain from this world
and take refuge in me alone;
I will wash away your every sin
and free you from every evil.
Never again will you grieve.

Fix your mind on me,
think of yourself as me;
worship me, sacrifice to me,
honor me as your own Self,
and you will surely come to me.
This I promise you,
for you are dear to me . . .

Arjuna!
Have you heard me?
Have my words hit their mark?

Arjuna
O Krishna,
Through your Grace,
the foe of delusion has been destroyed;
the clear light of wisdom has dawned.
I am now determined;
my every doubt is dispelled—
O Lord,
I stand here, ready,
To do as you command me.

Guru Gita

Parvati

O Lord, what is the Supreme Path
by which a bound soul
can become one with you?
Shower your grace on me, O Lord,
I place myself at your feet.

Lord Shiva

O goddess, I love you as my own Self.
Listen carefully—
The secret I am about to tell you
is well guarded in the three worlds;
do not reveal it to anyone
who lacks faith or devotion:

The Guru is Brahman,
Brahman is the Guru.
O beautiful one,
This is the truth.
This is the truth!

The Guru is not different
than the conscious Self;
The Guru is the Supreme Witness
within every creature.
Have no doubt about this.

GURU GITA

Salutations to the Guru—
The Guru is the Creator.
The Guru is the Sustainer.
The Guru is the Destroyer.
The Guru is indeed the Absolute Reality.

Salutations to the Guru—
The Supreme Cause of the universe,
The bridge across the ocean of this world,
The Master of all knowledge,
The Infinite Lord.

Salutations to the Guru—
By His reality the world is real,
By His light the mind is illumined,
By His joy all creatures are joyous.

Salutations to the Guru—
By His truth we exist,
By His brilliance the sun shines,
By His love sons and others are dear to us.

Guru Gita

With the Supreme knowledge of the Guru,
one comes to realize:
I am unborn,
Without decay, without beginning or end.
I am the Unchanging One,
The Consciousness and Bliss of the universe.
I am smaller than the smallest,
greater than the greatest.
I am beyond all beginnings,
Everlasting, Self-luminous,
Stainless, and pure.
I fill the supreme heavens.
I am immovable, blissful, and imperishable.

O Parvati,
It is true,
It is true,
What I tell you is true—
The Guru is the source
of all treasure in this universe;
Nothing is greater than the Guru,
No Truth can ever be more Supreme.

Vishnu Sahasranam

THE THOUSAND NAMES OF GOD

Om,
That One whose form is the entire universe:

That One is called *Vishnu,*
   The Supreme Being who
   enters everything and everyone.
Lord of all time,
Creator of all life,
Sustainer of all worlds,
He becomes everything in the universe
   without losing His pure existence.
He evolves and nourishes all creatures.
Indeed, He is the Supreme Self of every being.

That One is called *Shiva,*
   The Pure One.
Ever-free, without death or decay,
   He is the highest goal of liberated ones.
Witnessing everything
   without aid or instrument,
Steady, immovable, and changeless,
The source of all existence,
He is the one attainable through Yoga.

That One is called *Shambhu,*
    The bestower of supreme bliss.
Born of Her own free will,
    supporting the universe and its substratum,
    She exists of Herself, uncaused by another.

That One is called *Manu,*
    The only thinker in this universe.
One whose sight gives purity to everything,
    whose breath gives life to everything,
    whose lips give joy to everything.
He is The Supremely Auspicious One
    whose remembrance removes all obstacles.

That One is called *Kirti,*
    The root of all action,
    the sum total of all human achievement.
Eternal,
Requiring no other support,
She is the seed of the universe,
The one to whom all beings owe their existence.
"Where is She established, O Lord?—
    In Her own greatness itself."

That One is called *Sharma*,
    The Supreme Bliss.
Granting every object of desire,
Dwelling in all beings,
She is the one whose form
    cannot be measured by time or space;
She stands completely aside from all limitations.
Lord of all Lords,
    supremely tranquil,
There is no doubt—She is The Luminous One.

That One is called *Satya*,
    The Ever-Existing Truth.
Equally present in all beings,
Unlimited by any entity,
Standing free of all bondage,
She is the one whose every resolution comes true,
    whose worship always bear fruit.
O seeker,
    You will find Her seated in
    the lotus of your heart.

That One is called *Rudra*,
    The remover of all sorrow.
Knowing everything and shining everywhere,
Bestowing perfect knowledge of the universe,
Destroying all ignorance.
He is free from every defect,
The greatest of all good fortune,
He is the Supreme Destination,
    The attainment from which there is no return.

That one is called *Kavi,*
   The witness to the whole universe.
Purifying all those who adore Her,
Possessing infinite power,
Ruling everything within and without,
She is the one whose actions never go to waste,
Who dwells again and again
   as the incarnated soul.
She is the one who must be known
   by those who seek realization.

That One is called *Madhu,*
   The sweetness of love and bliss.
One whose illumination is brighter than all lights,
Whose strength is greater than all powers,
Whose wisdom surpasses all knowing.
Self-illumined,
The Spirit beyond all measure,
Endowed with greatness of every kind,
He bestows the highest destiny attainable
   to the pure of heart.

That One is called *Marishi,*
   The supreme virtue seen in realized beings.
The power of all worlds,
The remover of all fears,
The doer of all things,
He is the supreme brilliance,
The ultimate support,
The Father of all fathers.

Sages of Taoism

~

TAO TE CHING
CHUANG TZU
LIEH TZU

天下皆謂我道大似不肖夫唯大故似不
其細也夫我有三寶持而保之一曰慈二
敢爲天下先慈故能勇儉故能廣不敢爲
成器長今舍慈且勇舍儉且廣舍後且
先。

Between the sixth and third centuries B.C. the dominant philosophy in China was Confucianism, which stressed rules, responsibilities, and man's obligation to the social order. Although Confucianism offered a reassuring structure for civilized life—which is still present in Chinese society—it ignored the inner yearnings of the people for a more spiritual view of life. *Taoism* arose to fill this gap. This new philosophy put man back in touch with himself and the greater forces of the universe. Instead of emphasizing man's relationship to family and community, Taoism called on him to find a higher power within himself; instead of structure and rituals, the Taoist Sages taught simple living and flowing with nature. They believed that personal virtue, moral excellence, proper conduct, and kindness toward others were not meant to be learned, but would unfold naturally from that place of inner perfection.

Among the religious philosophies of the world, Taoism holds the distinct claim of being "soft": the All-Powerful Reality is praised for its weakness, not its strength; for being yielding and female, not dominant and male. Tao above all is fluid and alive; and a fundamental concept of Taoism is that the splendor of this world, and the greatness of Tao, is revealed through the natural flow of life.

The concept of Tao was first put forth in the **Tao Te Ching**, which now stands as the central text of Taoism. This short classic (*ching*) of only 5,000 words is a collection of sayings gathered from the writings of Chinese Sages between the sixth and second centuries B.C., and traditionally attributed to Lao Tzu. Blending together paradox, word play, mystical visions, spiritual counseling, and sound political advice, the *Tao Te Ching* tells of *Tao,* the Absolute Reality, and *Te,* how that Reality manifests. The simple yet profound teachings contained in this book have influenced every part of Chinese society—its philosophy, religion, art, medicine, and even its cooking. Recently the *Tao Te Ching* has gained great popularity in the West and ranks third only to the Bible and the *Bhagavad Gita* in English translations.

The other book that forms the backbone of Taoism is the **Chuang Tzu,** a fanciful collection of stories written by Chuang Tzu in the fourth century B.C. This bold and satirical piece of writing pokes fun at serious philosophers, parochial scholars, and all others who tend to hold back the boundless spirit of man. While the *Tao Te Ching* celebrates the virtue of humility, Chuang Tzu tells of freedom, of wandering the earth, of soaring through the inner skies. His work is so brilliant and convincing that even the scholars he slanders cannot help but secretly admire him. He was no doubt the greatest writer of the Chou Dynasty.

The **Lieh Tzu** is a minor collection of Taoist stories and parables said to have been written in the third century B.C. Although its author is unknown, by custom it is attributed to Lieh Yuk'ou.

TAO TE CHING

That which can be called the Tao
    is not the Eternal Tao
That which can be called the Name
    is not the Eternal Name

Tao is both Named and Nameless
As Nameless, it is
    the root of Heaven and Earth
As Named, it is
    the Mother of all things

A mind ever free of its own process
    beholds the true miracle of Tao
A mind ever lost in its own process
    sees only the forms of this world

Tao and this world seem different,
    but in truth they are one and the same
The only difference is in what we call them.

How deep and mysterious this unity is
    How profound, how great!
It is the truth beyond the truth,
    the mystery beyond the mind
It is the path to all wonder,
    the gate to the ecstatic nature of everything!

Tao Te Ching

Something formless, complete in itself
There before Heaven and Earth
Tranquil, vast, standing alone, unchanging
It provides for all things yet cannot be exhausted
It is the Mother of the Universe
I do not know its name
    so I call it "Tao"
Forced to name it further
I call it
    "Greater than the Greatest"
    "The End of all Endings"
I call it
    "That which is Beyond the Beyond"
    "That to which All Things Return"

Tao Te Ching

Eyes look but cannot see it
Ears listen but cannot hear it
Hands grasp but cannot touch it
Beyond the senses lies the great Unity—
    Invisible, Inaudible, Intangible

What rises up appears bright
What settles down appears dark
Yet there is neither darkness nor light
    just an unbroken dance of shadows
From nothingness to fullness
    and back again to nothingness
This formless form,
This imageless image
    cannot be grasped by mind or might
Try to face it
    In what place will you stand?
Try to follow it
    To what place will you go?

Know That which is beyond all beginnings
    And you will know everything right here and now
Know everything in this moment
    And you will know the Eternal Tao

Tao Te Ching

Without going out the door
    one can know the whole world
Without glancing out the window
    one can see the ways of Heaven
The further one goes
    the less one knows

Thus the Sage does not go, yet he knows
    He does not look, yet he sees
    He does not do, yet all is done

Tao Te Ching

Those who look down upon the world
   will surely take charge and try to change things
But this is a plan
   I've always seen fail
The world is Tao's own vessel
   It is Perfection manifest
It cannot be changed
It cannot be improved
For those who go on tampering, it's ruined
For those who try to grasp, it's gone

Allow your life to unfold naturally
Know that it too is a vessel of perfection
Just as you breathe in and breathe out
   Sometimes you're ahead and other times behind
   Sometimes you're strong and other times weak
   Sometimes you're in a crowd and other times alone

To the Sage
   all of life is but a movement toward perfection
So what need has he
   for the excessive, the extravagant, or the extreme?

Tao Te Ching

Again and again
Men come in with birth
   and go out with death
One in three are followers of life
One in three are followers of death
And those just passing from life to death
   also number one in three
But they all die in the end
Why is this so?
Because they all clutch to life
   and cling to this passing world

I hear that one who lives by his own truth
   is not like this
He walks without making footprints in this world
Going about, he does not fear the rhinoceros or tiger
Entering a battlefield, he does not fear sharp weapons
For in him the rhino can find no place to pitch its horn
The tiger no place to fix its claw
The soldier no place to thrust his blade
Why is this so?
Because he dwells in that place
   where death cannot enter

Tao Te Ching

Tao gives all things life
    Te gives them fulfillment
Nature is what shapes them
Living is what brings them to completion
Every creature honors Tao and worships Te
    not by force
    but by its own living and breathing

Tao gives all things life
    yet Te is what cultivates them
Te is the magic power that
    raises and rears them
    completes and prepares them
    comforts and protects them

To create without owning
To give without expecting
To fill without claiming
    This is the profound expression of Tao
    The perfect virtue of Te

Tao Te Ching

When life begins
 we are tender and weak
When life ends
 we are stiff and rigid
All things—the grass, the trees—
 in life are soft and pliant
 in death are dry and brittle

So the soft and supple
 are the companions of life
While the stiff and unyielding
 are the companions of death

An army that cannot yield
 will suffer defeat
A tree that cannot bend
 will crack in the wind
Thus by Nature's own decree
 the hard and strong are defeated
 while the soft and gentle are triumphant

TAO TE CHING

Nothing in this world
    is as soft and yielding as water
Yet for attacking the hard and strong
    none can triumph so easily
It is weak, yet none can equal it
It is soft, yet none can damage it
It is yielding, yet none can wear it away

Everyone knows that the soft overcomes the hard
    and the yielding triumphs over the rigid
Why then so little faith?
Why can no one practice it?

So the Sages say,
    Fulfill even the lowest position
    Love even the weakest creature
Then you will be called
    "Lord of every offering"
    "King of all below Heaven"

Tao Te Ching

"Surrender brings perfection"

The crooked are made straight
The empty are made full
The worn are made new
　　Have little and gain much
　　Have much and lose your way

So the Sage embraces the One
　　and comes to know the whole world
Not displaying himself, he shines forth
Not promoting himself, he is distinguished
Not claiming reward, he gains endless merit
Not seeking glory, his glory endures

The Sage knows how to follow
　　so he comes to command
He does not compete
　　so no one under Heaven can compete with him

The ancient saying,
　　"Surrender brings perfection,"
　　is not just an empty phrase
Truly, to the surrendered comes the perfect
　　To the perfect comes the whole Universe

TAO TE CHING

Hold fast to the Power of the One
It will unify the body
  and merge it with the spirit
It will cleanse the vision
  and reveal the world as flawless
It will focus the life-force
  and make one supple as a newborn

As you love the people and rule the state
  can you be selfless?
As the gates of Heaven open and close
  can you remain steady as a mother bird
  who sits with her nest?
As your wisdom reaches the four corners of the world
  can you keep the innocence of a beginner?

Know this Mysterious Power—
It guides without forcing
It serves without seeking reward
It brings forth and sustains life
  yet does not own or possess it

He who holds this Power
  brings Tao to this very Earth
He can triumph over the dragon's fire
  and the freeze of winter weather
Yet when he comes to rule the world
  it's with the gentleness of a feather

CHUANG TZU

The perfect man is a spiritual being,
    not bound by flesh.
Were the oceans to boil up around him,
    he would not feel hot;
Were the cosmos to freeze up in ice,
    he would not feel cold;
Were lightning to crack open the mountains,
    and fierce winds to heave the seas,
    he would not stir at all.

Such a being rides upon the clouds of heaven,
    mounts the sun and moon like a chariot,
    and passes with ease
    beyond the reaches of this world.
Neither life nor death can touch him—
    how much less so the concern over
    gain or loss?

CHUANG TZU

The Sage stands next to the Sun
    and the Moon
    while holding all of space and time
    in his hand.
He discards the confused and obscure;
    honors the meek and humble;
    and blends everything
        into a universal whole.
As men toil on to obtain some reward,
    he appears listless and dull.
For he has merged all things
    into perfect purity.
And from this purity
    he can vanquish the disparities
    of ten thousand ages
    in a single moment.

On and on goes his delight;
Should the whole of creation
    come to an end,
    his delight
    would go on still.

CHUANG TZU

When Tzu-ch'i of Nan-po was taking a stroll by the Hill of Shang he spotted a great tree that towered above all the rest. Its branches could shelter a thousand horses and its shade would easily cover them all. "What kind of tree is this," he thought, "its timber must be quite extraordinary." But when looking up he discovered that the higher branches were too gnarled to be used for floorboards or rafters. When looking down he noticed that the trunk was too soft and pitted to be used for coffins. He licked one of the leaves and it left a burning taste in his mouth. He sniffed the bark and the odor was enough to take away his appetite for three days. "This wretched tree is completely useless," he exclaimed, "and this must be why it has grown so large! Aha!—this is the exact kind of uselessness that the holy man puts to great use."

CHUANG TZU

Master Carpenter Ch'ing set out to carve a piece of wood into a large horse. When the horse was completed, all those who looked at it were amazed, thinking that at any moment it would burst to life and run off. Surely, they thought, this must be the handiwork of the gods themselves. When the Prince of Lu saw the horse he asked, "What is the secret of your art?"

"What secret?" Ch'ing replied, "I am but a simple craftsman. There is one thing, however. Before I set about carving I guard against anything that would diminish my vital force. I keep all distractions at a distance and my mind becomes very still. After three days in this state, I lose all thought of reward or personal benefit. After five days, I no longer care about praise or blame, or of what it takes to make a good or bad carving. After seven days I lose all notion that these are my hands or that this body belongs to me. I don't even know why I am making this horse or for whom. My skill is focused on but one thing; all disturbance of the outer world is gone. It is only then that I enter the forest in search of the right tree. I find one of exquisite form. Seeing the horse captured within the folds of the grain, struggling to get out, I set my hand to the chisel so as to free it. If this is not your approach, what will you accomplish, why keep everyone up at night with the banging of your chisel?"

"You see it is very simple: I just bring my own nature into harmony with that of the wood, then I begin. Whatever is not in harmony, I carve away. What people suspect is the work of some supernatural force is no more than this."

CHUANG TZU

Confucius once returned from a visit to Lao Tzu and was asked by his disciples:

"Master, in what ways did you debate with Lao Tzu?"

Confucius replied:

I have seen the fierce tiger caged, the great tortoise snared, even the swiftest bird felled by an arrow, yet when I visited the House of Chou I saw a dragon—a dragon by which some miracle had fashioned a body; by which blazing heat shines forth color; by which riding upon the clouds of heaven the two principles of creation are nourished. That dragon was Lao Tzu. My mouth was agape; I could not talk. Tell me then, how was I supposed to debate with him?

Chuang Tzu

A philosopher once came to discuss the rules of proper conduct with Lao Tzu, and got this reply:

> If when winnowing chaff, the dust blows in your eyes, how can you find true direction? If a swarm of mosquitoes is biting you at night, how are you to get any sleep? So let me tell you, all this talk of "benevolence" and "goodness to one's neighbor" is nothing but an annoyance which only confuses the mind and keeps people up at night! Just let the world hold to its own nature. Let the wind blow as it may. And you—just follow your own nature. Surely these virtues you talk about will come and establish themselves. Wherefore this self-defeating effort, as if searching for a runaway son while beating on a loud drum?
>
> The swan is white without a daily bath; the crow is black without the need to color itself. Can we argue whether white is fitting to the swan or black to the crow? Can fame, or the learning of proper conduct, add anything to the greatness which a man already possesses? When the water dries up, the fish are left on the ground with nothing but the spittle from their mouths to moisten each other; tell me, can this compare to leaving them in their own native rivers and lakes?
>
> Alas then—be off! You are disturbing the nature of man with all your talk!

CHUANG TZU

Some day comes the Great Awakening
   when we realize
   that this life
   is no more than a dream.
Yet the foolish go on thinking
   they are awake:
Surveying the panorama of life
   with such clarity,
   they call this one a prince
   and that one a peasant—
What delusion!
The great Confucius and you
   are both a dream.
And I, who say all this is a dream,
   I, too, am a dream.

What mystery this vision contains!

Someday a great Sage will come
   and explain it to us,
But that may not be
   until ten thousand generations
   have come and gone.
Still, for us in this dream,
   it will only seem
   like the passing
   of a single morning or afternoon.

I did not know whether I was Chuang Tzu dreaming I was a butterfly; or a butterfly dreaming I was Chuang Tzu.

LIEH TZU

When Yin Sheng heard of Lieh Tzu's ability to ride on the wings of the wind, he immediately set off to become his disciple. After only a few days with the Sage, Yin Sheng pleaded for initiation into the secret arts; ten times he asked, and ten times he received no answer. Yin Sheng finally lost his patience and went to bid the Master farewell. Lieh Tzu said to him:

Why this impatience? Why all this coming and going? Sit down already and I will tell you something about my own Master: After I served him for three years, my mind was calm and no longer reflected on right or wrong, my lips were still and no longer spoke of gain or loss. Then, for the first time, my Master glanced at me—nothing more.

After five years of service, something shifted: my mind was filled with thoughts of right and wrong, and my lips kept talking about gain and loss. Then, for the first time, my Master's face softened and he smiled at me.

After seven years of service there was another shift: I let my mind entertain what thoughts it may, but it no longer had thoughts of right or wrong. I let my lips talk about whatever they wanted to, but there was not another word about gain or loss. Then, and only then, my Master asked me to come sit by his side.

After nine years of service my mind merged back into its own source, my lips spoke only words of truth. I knew nothing about right or wrong, gain or loss. I knew nothing about Master or disciple—for I could no longer tell the difference. Inside and outside had merged into One. No longer was there a distinction between eye and ear, ear and nose, nose and mouth—all were the same. My mind was silent, my body had dissolved; my flesh and my bones melted into nothingness. I was totally unaware of having a body, or what was under my feet. Suddenly I was carried up by the hands of the wind—flying this way and that—like dry chaff or a falling leaf. I floated up through the skies not knowing whether I was riding the wind or whether the wind was riding me!

One day, Yin Sheng, you too will learn how to fly, but first you must learn how to stay in one place on this earth.

BUDDHIST MASTERS

—

SHAKYAMUNI BUDDHA
THE DHAMMAPADA
EIHEI DOGEN
BASSUI ZENJI
HUANG PO
SHANTIDEVA
YUNG-CHIA
GIZAN

The Sanskrit word *Buddha* means "the Awakened One," and the religion of Buddhism is born of the final awakening of **Shakyamuni Buddha** (?563–?483 B.C.), also known as Siddhartha Gautama. The basic tenet put forth by Buddha was that life brings suffering, that suffering has its roots in desire, and that by systematic practice desire can be destroyed and Nirvana—a state of bliss beyond all suffering—can be reached.

Buddha was born as a prince of the Shakyas in a small kingdom at the foot of the Himalayas; he enjoyed every luxury. One day he ventured beyond the sheltered walls of the palace where he was shocked to see death, sickness, and the misery of the world. Soon after he left his comfortable surroundings to find a way to overcome the inevitable suffering of worldly existence. After years of meditation and severe austerities, he attained enlightenment under the now famed bodhi (enlightenment) tree. A small Canon attributed to Buddha is the **Dhammapada,** a brilliant collection of short and penetrating verses that gives the essence of Buddha's teachings; it is regarded, in every school of Buddhism, as a masterpiece of spiritual literature.

The school of Zen Buddhism stresses the importance of enlightenment and the knowing of one's own mind through the practice of *zazen,* a thought-free, sitting meditation. A great Chinese Zen master and a forefather of the Rinzai school of Zen was **Huang Po** (d. 850). Rinzai stresses the use of a *koan*—a confounding riddle that cannot be answered by the intellect—to bring the student beyond the mind into a state of sudden realization. Huang Po is also famous for his non-dual philosophy called *Doctrine of the One Mind*.

The Chinese Master, **Yung-chia** (665–713) was said to have been in a state of perfect repose while "walking, standing, sitting, and lying down." According to legend, he visited the Zen Patriarch Hui-neng and attained complete realization in one night; and so he was called "master of the enlightenment attained in one night." His most popular work on Zen is a set of verses called *The Song of Enlightenment*.

Shantideva (7th century) was a follower of Mahayana Buddhism, a school that emphasizes the pursuit of enlightenment for the benefit of all mankind, not simply for the individual's sake. His text, *Entering the Path of Enlightenment*, is still widely used by the Buddhists of Tibet.

The most important Zen Master, and considered Japan's greatest religious figure, was **Eihei Dogen** (1200–1253). He was the founder of the Soto School of Zen, which emphasizes the attainment of gradual enlightenment through a pure form of meditation, called *shikan-taza*—an alert, thought-free state of awareness, directed to no object, and empty of all content. This heightened consciousness was called by one master, "the mind of somebody facing death." Dogen's principle work, the *Shobogenzo,* is regarded as a true classic of Zen literature.

Japanese Zen Master **Bassui Zenji** (1327–1387) was a young boy when his father died, and the intense grief he felt led him to question his own nature and go in search of a Master. During his quest he never stayed overnight in a temple as traditional pilgrims and seekers did, but instead made his home in isolated huts where he would practice long hours of *zazen* and ponder his own *koan,* "Who is the Master?" He finally met his Master, Koho Zenji, and reach enlightenment.

Later, at the age of fifty, Bassui Zenji took on disciples as abbot of a large monastery.

Gizan (1802–1878) was a lesser-known Zen Master whose insightful poetry and bold teaching style endeared him to all his followers.

SHAKYAMUNI BUDDHA

The ocean has only one taste, the taste of salt.
Truth has only one taste, the taste of liberation.

Siddhartha was tempted by the illusive power of Maya and
replied:

Why do you tempt me, Maya?
What will I do with the pleasures you offer,
I who have faith?
    I struggle in faith, evil one,
    My faith is my life.
For look, my faith, like a burning wind
Drying up rivers,
    will dry up my blood,
    will dry up everything that flows.
Till blood, bile, and phlegm dry up,
I shall sit here,
    with tranquil mind,
    and steady wisdom.

Faith is my weapon. Powerless
Against it is your army, O temptress.
Bring Lust and Restlessness,
Hunger and Thirst,
Sloth, Cowardice, Doubt, Hypocrisy—
All powerless.

SHAKYAMUNI BUDDHA

Consider carefully the things I have taught and the things I have not taught.

I have not taught that the world is eternal. I have not taught that the world is not eternal. I have not taught that the world is finite. I have not taught that the world is infinite. I have not taught that the soul and the body are the same. I have not taught that the soul and the body are different. I have not taught that the liberated person exists after death. I have not taught that he does not exist after death . . .

Why have I not taught all this? Because all this is useless, it has nothing to do with real Truth: it does not lead to cessation of passion, to peace, to supreme wisdom, to the holy life, or to Nirvana. That is why I have not taught all this.

And what have I taught? I have taught that suffering exists, that suffering has an origin, that suffering has an end.

Why have I taught this? Because this is useful, it has to do with real Truth: it leads to the cessation of passion, it brings peace, supreme wisdom, the holy life, and Nirvana. That is why I have taught all this.

Therefore, consider carefully what I have taught and what I have not taught.

SHAKYAMUNI BUDDHA

Buddha picked up a flower and showed it to the assembled people. They did not understand. Only Mahakashyapa smiled.

Buddha said, "I have in my hand the doctrine of right action: birthless, deathless, formless, inscrutable. It is beyond sacred texts; it does not need words to explain it. I give it to Mahakashyapa."

THE DHAMMAPADA

TWIN VERSES

The mind, the mind, the mind—
This is the beginning and the end of it all.
The quality of one's life depends on
    nothing but the mind:
If one's words or deeds come from an impure mind
    then suffering surely follows.
If one's words and deeds come from a pure mind
    then happiness walks with him as his own shadow.

How can such thoughts as,
"He abused me, he cheated me, he robbed me"
    release one from the snares of anger?
Hatred is never banished by hatred,
Hatred is banished only by love.
This is a law that has never changed.

We are guests in this world,
    here for only a short while.
Those who know this truth do not waste their time
    with quibbling or gossip.

Living only for pleasure,
    stuffing oneself with this and that,
    being lazy and undisciplined—
This makes one powerless.
Maya's illusion blows him about
    like a twig blown about in a storm.

One who chooses the beneficial over the pleasurable,
Who has his senses under control,
Who has faith and puts forth effort—
He is a mountain.
He stands unshaken by the winds of this world . . .

As rain seeps through a poorly thatched roof,
Passion seeps through a poorly trained mind.
As rain is held back by a well-thatched roof,
Passion is held back by a well-trained mind.

Those who know all the scriptures,
But do not live by them,
Have no share in the holy life.
They are like a cowherd,
Counting someone else's cattle.
Those who know just a few lines from the scriptures,
And live by them!—
    Harboring only good thoughts,
    Banishing lust, hatred, and delusion;
    Wanting nothing from this world or the next—
They have a full share in the holy life.

THE SAINT

His journey is over!
All sorrow is gone,
Every shackle undone,
He is completely free.

Those yearning to be free
    are not content to remain in one place.
They are ever-striving for a way
    to pass beyond this world,
Like swans leaving their lake
    to fly upward to the sky.

Who can trace the path of these great ones?
These beings who are pure at heart,
    not swayed by the senses,
    living without attachment,
    and accepting of whatever life gives them?

More difficult than following the flight of birds
    is it to follow these beings,
These great ones who wander through the infinite skies
    with absolute freedom.

Even the gods envy them:
Their senses controlled like a well-trained horse,
Their souls free from pride and jealousy.
These great beings welcome everyone like the earth,
Are steadfast like a stone foundation,

Pure like the waters of a lake,
And no longer bound by birth or death.
Perfect wisdom has filled them with peace:
Their every thought, word, and action
    are in perfect harmony with the universe.

Having seen the Eternal Truth
All falsehood has vanished,
All bonds have been cut,
All desires have been conquered.
They are indeed the kings among men.

Holy is the place where such great ones dwell.
They fill with delight the village and the forest,
    the valley and the hill;
They fill with delight
    every place in this world.

THE DHAMMAPADA

THE THOUSANDS

Better than a thousand useless words
Is one word which brings peace.
　　Better than a thousand useless verses
　　Is one line which brings joy.
　　　　Better than a thousand useless poems
　　　　Is one poem which brings love.

One day of contemplation
Is better than a hundred years of thoughtlessness.
　　One day of wisdom
　　Is better than a hundred years of ignorance.
　　　　One day of effort
　　　　Is better than a hundred years of laziness.

True devotion to a Master
Is better than a hundred years of worship,
　　and a thousand joyless rituals.

True devotion to a Master
Is better than dwelling in the forest a hundred years
　　and tending a thousand sacred fires.

True devotion to a Master
Is better than anything—
Long life, beauty, happiness, strength.

Eihei Dogen

Do not practice Buddha's way for your own sake. Do not practice Buddha's way for name and gain. Do not practice Buddha's way to attain blissful reward. Do not practice Buddha's way to attain marvelous effects. Practice Buddha's way solely for the sake of Buddha's way. This is Buddha's way.

A teacher of old said, "If the beginning is not right, a thousand practices will be useless."

How true these words are! Practice of the way depends on whether the guiding master is a true teacher or not.

The disciple is like wood, and the teacher resembles a craftsman. Even if the wood is good, without a skilled craftsman its extraordinary beauty is not revealed. Even if the wood is bent, placed in skilled hands its splendid merits immediately appear. By this you should know that realization is genuine or false depending on whether the teacher is true or incompetent.

Bassui Zenji

Fear nothing but the failure to experience your True-nature. This is Zen practice.

If you would free yourself from the sufferings of birth and death, you must learn the direct way to become a Buddha. This way is no other than the realization of your own Mind. . . . If you want to realize your own Mind, you must first of all look into the source from which thoughts flow. Sleeping and working, standing and sitting, profoundly ask yourself, "What is my own Mind?" with an intense yearning to resolve this question. This searching of one's own mind leads ultimately to enlightenment.

A Buddha has never existed who has not realized this Mind, and every last being within the Six Realms of Experience is perfectly endowed with it.

Bassui Zenji

Imagine a child sleeping next to its parents and dreaming it is being beaten or is painfully sick. The parents cannot help the child no matter how much it suffers. . . . If the child could awaken itself, it could be freed of this suffering automatically. In the same way, one who realizes that his own Mind is Buddha, frees himself instantly from sufferings arising from the ceaseless change of birth-and-death. If a Buddha could prevent it, do you think he would allow even one sentient being to fall into hell?

What is obstructing realization? Nothing but your own half-hearted desire for truth. Think of this and exert yourself to the utmost.

HUANG PO

All the Buddhas and all sentient beings are nothing but the Universal Mind, besides which nothing exists. This Mind which has always existed is unborn and indestructible. It is not green nor yellow, and has neither form nor appearance. It does not belong to the categories of things that exist or do not exist, nor can it be reckoned as being new or old. It is neither long nor short, big nor small, for it transcends all limits, measures, names, speech, and every method of treating it concretely.

The Universal Mind alone is the Buddha and there is no distinction between the Buddha and sentient beings, except that sentient beings are attached to forms and so seek externally for Buddhahood. By their very seeking for it they lose it. . . . If they could only put a stop to their conceptual thoughts they would realize that the Buddha is directly before them.

Huang Po

Countless as the sands of the Ganges are the merits that come from performing the six perfect duties and vast number of similar practices. But since you are fundamentally complete in every respect, you should not try to supplement that perfection by such meaningless practices. When there is occasion for them, perform them, and when the occasion has passed, remain quiescent. If you are not absolutely convinced that the Mind is the Buddha, and if you are attached to forms, practices, and meritorious deeds, your way of thinking is false and quite contrary to the Way. Your mind *is* the Buddha! There is no other Buddha! There is no other Mind!

HUANG PO

Our original Buddha-Nature is, in highest truth, devoid of any trace of objectivity. It is void, omnipresent, silent, pure; it is glorious and mysterious; peaceful and joyous—and that is all. Enter deeply in it by awakening to it yourself. That which is before you is it in all its entirety, with nothing whatsoever lacking. Even if you go through all the stages of a Bodhisattva's progress toward Buddhahood, one by one—when at last, in a single flash, you attain to full realization—you will only be realizing your original Buddha-Nature which has been with you all the time. By all the foregoing stages you will not have added a single thing to it. You will merely regard those ages of work and achievement as nothing but unreal actions performed in a dream. That is why the Buddha said: "I truly attained nothing from complete, unexcelled enlightenment."

Do not permit the events of your daily lives to bind you, but never withdraw from them. Only by acting thus can you earn the title of "A Liberated One."

SHANTIDEVA

The pain that wins me the enlightenment is of brief term; it is like the pain of cutting out a buried arrow to heal its smart. All physicians restore health by painful courses; then to undo much suffering let us bear a little. But even this fitting course the Great Physician has not enjoined upon us; he heals those who are greviously sick by the most tender treatment.

Eager to escape sorrow, men rush into sorrow; from desire of happiness they blindly slay their own happiness; their hunger for happiness brings them only more and more pain. Whence shall come one so kind as to satisfy them with all manner of happiness, allay their pains, and shatter their delusion? Whence comes such a friend?

YUNG-CHIA

One Nature,
    perfect and pervading,
    circulates in all natures.
One Reality,
    all-knowing,
    contains within itself all realities.
The one moon is reflected
    wherever there is a sheet of water,
And all the moons in all the waters
    are embraced within the one moon.
The embodied Truth of all the Buddhas
    enters into my own being,
And my own being is found in union with theirs.

The Inner Light is beyond both praise and blame,
Like unto space it knows no boundaries;
Yet it is right here with us,
    ever retaining its serenity and fullness.
It is only when you seek it that you lose it.
You cannot take hold of it nor can you get rid of it;
While you can do neither, it goes on its own way.
You remain silent and it speaks;
    you speak and it is silent.
The Gate of Heaven is wide open
    with not a single obstruction before it.

YUNG-CHIA

"No" is not necessarily "no," nor is "yes" necessarily
   "yes."
But when you miss even a tenth of an inch,
   the difference widens up to a thousand miles.
When it is "yes,"
   a young native girl attains Buddhahood in an instant.
When it is "no,"
   the greatest living scholar falls into hell.

The mind is the author of all works
   and the body the sufferer of all ills.

GIZAN

Coming and going,
  life and death.
A thousand villages,
  a million houses.
Don't you get the point?
Moon in the water,
  blossom in the sky.

WISDOM OF THE HEBREWS

—

BOOK OF PSALMS
WISDOM OF SOLOMON
ECCLESIASTICUS

מְשׁוּרָה תִּשְׁתֶּה, וְעַל
זֶל. אִם אַתָּה עוֹשֶׂ
וֹב לְךָ לָעוֹלָם הַבָּא
משנה ה. אַל תְּבַ
לְמוֹדְךָ עֲשֵׂה, וְאַל
שֶׁלְחָנָם, וְכִתְרְךָ גְּדוֹ
ד שְׂכַר פְּעֻלָּתֶךָ.
משנה ו. גְּדוֹלָה תּ
נִית בִּשְׁלֹשִׁים מַעַל
נִית בְּאַרְבָּעִים וּשְׁמ
עֲרִיכַת שְׂפָתַיִם, בִּנ
טָהֳרָה, בְּשִׁמּוּשׁ חֲכ

The Hebrew Scriptures are an extensive body of literature that trace the early history and spiritual unfoldment of a small but determined people. The genius of these early Hebrew Sages, and the sweeping expression of their religious zeal, colors every page of this exalted work. The most familiar and widely used book of the Bible is the **Book of Psalms** (10th–3rd century B.C.), a collection of sacred songs which has been aptly called, "the immortal song-book of the human heart." Through its 150 verses, it captures the feeling and spirit of the entire Old Testament: tracing Jewish history and the essential teachings of the prophets, honoring the Law, and running the gamut of religious feeling—from anguish and despair to devotion, faith, and love for God. Because of its rich spirituality and depth of religious feeling, the Book of Psalms are embraced by all people and form a common ground for the Jewish and Christian faiths. Although the author of the Psalms is unknown, about half the verses are attributed to King David.

Five books of the Bible—Proverbs, Ecclesiastes, Job, the Wisdom of Solomon, and Ecclesiasticus (the Wisdom of Sirach)—make up what is known as the Wisdom Literature. This group of writings is filled with pithy sayings, universal teachings, spiritual insights, and praises of the creative power of God known as *Sophia,* or Wisdom. **Ecclesiasticus** (180 B.C.) was written in Hebrew by Jeshua ibn Sirach of Jerusalem. Its ethical outlook, wit, keen observation, and use of parallel couplets gives it a close resemblance to Proverbs. The **Wisdom of Solomon** (?50 B.C.) was written in Greek by an unknown Jew living in Alexandria and offers a true fusion of Greek and Jewish thought. By custom, however, it is ascribed to a hero of the past: King Solomon (10th century B.C.).

Both Ecclesiasticus and the Wisdom of Solomon are found in a portion of the Bible called the *Apocrypha,* a Greek word meaning "hidden" or "obscure," which later came to mean "dubious" or "unauthorized." Although of Jewish origin, the writings of the *Apocrypha* were rejected as part of the Jewish canon because of their late date—written during the interval between the end of the Old Testament and the beginning of the New Testament—and because they do not claim Divine revelation as their source. The Roman Catholic Church, however, judged them valid and included them in its official Bible, placed between the Old and New Testaments. The King James Version of 1611 also followed this practice.

Both books give a brilliant, personal, and poetic account of God's feminine aspect. This creative power, supreme intelligence, and wisdom inherent in man, was called *Shekinah* by the Jewish mystics, and to the Greeks of a later time, She became *Sophia,* their word for "wisdom." In these books, *Sophia* is described as "pervading and permeating all things"; as "the source of all treasure in the universe"; and She herself says, "every people and nation are under my sway." It may be that The Wisdom Literature was banned from the Jewish canon, not due to a lack of inspiration, but because of the danger that this Supreme female Spirit might become a second and separate Divinity, thus threatening the Jewish insistence that there is only one God. As it says in the book of Isaiah, "I am the Lord, there is no other. I, the Lord, do all things."

PSALM 23

The Lord is my shepherd,
I shall not want.
He brings me to where the grass is green
    and leads me to where the waters are still.
I drink—and I am filled with life!

All I do is call out His Name
    and the right path appears before me.
Even though I walk through this world,
    where the shadow of death falls on everyone,
I fear no harm—
    for He is always with me,
    His staff is always ready to protect me.
In this place filled with hunger
    the Lord has spread out a table of delights
    and bathed my head in scented oil.
My heart is filled with His Love;
Goodness and Purity will follow me
    every day of my life.

Although appearing like others,
    I do not live in this world of men:
I live in the Lord's house,
    and am forever in His keeping.

Book of Psalms

PSALM 119

How blessed are those whose way is pure,
    who walk along the path you have shown them.
How blessed are those who hear your voice,
    who seek your care with all their hearts.
I pray that my ways please you,
    that they be set according to your ways.

My soul cleaves to the dust;
    my eyes stare into the night.
O giver of life!
I have prayed, and you have answered;
I have wept, and you have given me strength.
O Lord, remove the darkness from my soul
    and show me the light of your truth.

May your love and kindness find shelter
    in the depths of my heart.
May your word be my salvation.
O Lord, do not take the truth from my lips,
    keep it with me
    so I may sing your glory forever.

I will walk freely, speaking to all who seek your wisdom;
I will tell of your miracle to kings and princes,
    and I will not be daunted.
I will delight in your wisdom,

I will reach out my hand for your touch,
    and I will hold on to your every word.
How great is my fortune,
How great are the gifts that come from you.

Your hands made me and fashioned me;
    show me the truth,
    and the wisdom to know your will.
Let the people who love you see me and be glad;
    for they will know that I am your messenger;
    that I come to speak your words.

O Lord, I know that every hardship along the way
    is for me to grow in your love.
May I find delight in all you give me,
May I comfort all those who turn in my direction,
May my joy be complete
    and your Name forever on my lips.

My soul longs to know you again;
I stand here hoping for a sign,
    hoping for a thread to hold on to . . .
My sight has grown dim searching for you.
When will you come?
When will you show yourself to me?
I may shrivel up like a wineskin,
I may be hounded by countless lies,
I may be swept from the face of this earth,
    but I will never turn away from you.
What was I born for if not to follow you?
What is there to live for if not your undying love?
O Lord come alive in my heart—

Come alive so that we may,
    once again,
    be as one.

O Lord, your Word is eternal.
It is fixed in the heavens,
It stands as firm as the earth,
It has fulfilled the prayers of every generation.
O Lord, without the strength that comes
    from your Name,
    I surely would have perished long ago.

I will never forget your teachings,
    for through them you have come alive within me.
I may see the heavens fall,
I may see the earth crumble,
I may see all creation come to an end,
    but I will stand, forever here,
    as your servant.

O Lord, I hold your love with me all the time.
It makes me strong,
It cuts through my doubts,
It gives me great insight
    and the wisdom of a sage,
It keeps me on the right path.
How sweet is your love to my taste,
    sweeter than honey to my lips!
O Lord what is there without your love?
Without your love there is nothing
    but the taste of bitterness.

O Lord, you are a lamp to my feet,
  a light on my path.
Wherever you go, there I have sworn to follow.
I know the way may be steep
    and the journey filled with pain,
    but every step of the way
    you will give me strength.
O Lord, how can I ever hope to repay you?
All I can offer is folded hands
    and the readiness to do as you bid me.
You are my everlasting inheritance;
    you are the joy of my life.
I stand here resolved, to do as you command,
To follow the path
    that leads me back to you.

Thou art my shield and my hiding place.
Thou art my sole protector.
Thou art my only support.
O Lord, banish all evil from my mind
    and replace it with the yearning to know you.
Give me faith and humility
    and keep me free from harm.
What use is this life without you?
You are all that is safe,
    you are all that is true.

All my life I have looked for you.
Could you let these eyes fail
    before they have rested upon your form?
Could you forsake me in that way?
O Lord, be kind to your servant—

show yourself to me.
This is my truth, this is my life,
    this is what I want more
    than all the world has to offer.

Every word that comes from your lips
    fills me with wonder.
And here I sit, waiting to do as you bid me.
Your words shine;
    they illumine those in despair;
    they give understanding to the simple.
I am out of breath calling for you. . . .
Turn in my direction
    and fill me with your grace.
I am knocking—answer:
    for this is the promise
    you have given to all those who love you.
O Lord, fulfill your promise—
    keep my feet on the path that leads to your glory.
Do not let anything take me away.
Let the glory of your splendor
    be seen by this servant of yours . . .
If I go my own way
    and do not follow your laws
    then let me suffer,
    let me wail,
    let my eyes run down with a flood of tears.

I cry out with my whole heart—answer me, O Lord!
Save me, from this ocean of darkness.
Show me the way out.
I rise before dawn and wait to hear your voice.
My eyes stay open past the midnight watch,
    so that I might come to know all you have taught me.

You are so near my Lord;
    you are the eternal support;
    you are the Supreme goal . . .
I have but one prayer:
    that every step I take
    be a step toward you.

My heart stands in awe of you,
    and I am filled with joy whenever I hear your Name.
Seven times a day I praise thee;
    seven times a day I remember the justice of your care.
Those who love everything you give,
    find great peace,
    and nothing causes them to stumble.
Here I am, do with me as you will,
    for all my life lies open before thee.

Let these tears of mine reach you,
    let these supplications be seen by you.
Let my tongue sing of your glory,
    and let my life be a testimony of your kindness . . .

O Lord, where is my salvation?
Where is this life bringing me?
If I go astray like a lost sheep, look for me.
Look for me O Lord!
For I am your servant;
    I am the one who will never forget you,
    I am the one who will never forget your love.

Wisdom of Solomon

Sophia is the Supreme Spirit devoted to the good of all people . . .

She shines bright in the gloom of ignorance;
She is unfading;
    easily seen by those who love Her;
    easily found by those who look for Her,
And quickly does She come
    to those who seek Her help.

One who rises early,
    intent on finding Her,
    will not grow weary of the quest—
For one day he will find Her seated in his own heart.

To set all one's thoughts on Her
    is true wisdom,
And to be ever aware of Her
    is the sure way to perfect peace.
For Sophia Herself goes about in search
    of those who are worthy of Her;
With every step She comes to guide them;
    in every thought She comes to meet them.

Wisdom of Solomon

The true beginning of spiritual life is the desire to know
  Sophia;
A desire to know Her brings one to love Her;
Loving Her enables one to follow Her will;
Following Her will is the sure path to immortality;
And immortality is oneness with God.
So the desire to know Sophia
  leads to God and His Kingdom—
  a never-fading Kingdom.
With all your thrones and scepters
  you may rule the world for a while,
But take hold of Sophia
  and you will rule the world forever.

WISDOM OF SOLOMON

I, too, am a mortal man, like all of you,
Descended from the first born,
Formed out of the earth in
    my mother's womb . . .
When I was born, I breathed in the common air,
    was laid upon the ground,
    and wailed out a cry as all others do.
No king begins life in any other way;
For everyone comes into this world by one path
    and by the same path they go out again.

Seeing this predicament, I prayed,
    and wisdom was given to me;
I called for help,
    and the Supreme Spirit, Sophia,
    answered me.
I valued Her above scepter and throne . . .
Next to Her, all the gold in the world
    seemed like a handful of sand,
    and all the silver like a pile of dirt.
I loved Her more than health and beauty,
    and preferred Her to the light of day;
For Her radiance never fades
    and Her light never sets.

With Her comes all good things,
    and She carries in Her arms
    wealth beyond counting.
I rejoiced with love for all people,
    as I could see Sophia in their hearts,
    guiding them.

What I learned with great effort
    I now share freely;
    I do not hoard Her wealth for myself.
She is an inexhaustible treasure for mankind;
She blesses the world with Supreme wisdom,
    and allows all people to realize
    their unity with God.
She is the Supreme Spirit:
All-knowing and sacred;
One, yet pervading many,
    subtle, ever-free, lucid,
    stainless, clear, and invincible;
She is the love of goodness,
    ever-ready, unobstructed,
    beneficent, kindly toward all,
    steadfast, unerring, and untouched by care.
She is all-powerful, the witness of all,
    and found in those
    who are wise, pure-hearted, and humble.

WISDOM OF SOLOMON

Sophia moves more easily than motion itself;
By reason of Her purity
 She permeates all things.
She is like a fine mist
 rising from the power of God,
The divine radiance
 streaming from the glory of the Almighty;
Nothing can stain Her immaculate purity.
She is the shimmering glow of everlasting Light,
The flawless mirror of God's Power on earth,
The Supreme image of all good things.

Though one, She becomes everything;
 from within Herself, by Her own power,
She makes all things new;
Age after age She enters into holy souls,
 making them perfect,
 and leading them back to God.
For God only accepts those
 who have made their home with Sophia.
She is fairer than the sun,
 and greater than every constellation;
She is more radiant than the light of day—
 for day is overcome by night,
 but against Sophia no darkness can prevail.
Her power spans this world from end to end,
 and keeps all things in perfect harmony.

Wisdom of Solomon

Sophia I loved;
I sought Her out in my youth,
I fell in love with Her beauty,
    and I longed to make Her my bride.
All glory is born of Her,
    for She is one with God;
The Lord of all things
    loves Her as Himself.
She is the Supreme Power of initiation,
    imparting the secret knowledge of God,
    and carrying out all His works.
If wealth is desired,
    what wealth could be greater than Sophia,
    the source of all treasure in the universe?

But I saw that my efforts were useless:
Only through the gift of God
    could I have Her for my own.
My understanding was such
    that I knew at least this much.
And so I pleaded with the Lord,
    and prayed from the deepest reaches of my heart:

O Lord, God of our Fathers,
Whose Word has made all things,
Whose wisdom fills every heart with righteousness;
O Lord, O merciful Lord,
Grant me that one who sits by your throne—
Grant me Sophia.

ECCLESIASTICUS

Hear the praise of Sophia from Her own mouth:

"I am the Word that was first uttered by the Most High;
It was I who covered the earth like a mist.
My dwelling-place was in the high heaven;
my throne was in a pillar of cloud.
Alone I made a circuit of the sky
and traversed the depth of the abyss.
The waves of the sea, the whole earth,
all people and nations are under my sway . . .
Before time began He created me,
and I shall remain forever.
In this world I manifest His presence . . .
It was He who established me in the city He loved
and gave me rule over Jerusalem.
I took root in the hearts of those honored by the Lord,
those chosen to be His special possession.
And there I grew like the cedars of Lebanon,
Like the cypress on the slopes of Hermon,
Like the date-palms at Engedi,
Like the roses at Jericho.
I grew like a fair olive tree in the vale;
like a plane-tree planted beside the water.
Like cassia or camel-thorn I was redolent of spices,
and spread my fragrance like choice myrrh . . .
I was like the smoke of incense in the sacred tent.
Like terebinth I spread out my branches,
laden with honor and grace.
I put forth lovely shoots like a vine,
and my blossoms were a harvest
        of love, reverence, knowledge, and holy hope.

Come to me, you who desire me,
and eat your fill of my fruit.
The memory of me is sweeter than syrup,
the possession of me sweeter than honey dripping from the
   comb.

ECCLESIASTICUS

All of Sophia belongs to the Lord
   and She is with Him forever.
Who can count the sands of the sea,
the drops of rain, or the days of unending time?
Who can measure the height of the sky,
the breadth of the earth, or the depth of the abyss?
Sophia was the first of all created things;
intelligent purpose has been there from the beginning.
Who has unraveled the mystery of Sophia?
Who has understood Her subtlety?
One alone,
   the Lord most magnificent and wise.
He created Her,
He watches and delights in Her,
He infuses Her into every part of creation,
Giving Her, in some measure, to all mankind,
   yet in full to those who love Him.

Sophia raises Her sons to greatness
and cares for all those who seek Her.
To love Her is to love life;
To serve Her is to serve the Holy One,
To rise early for Her sake is to be filled with joy . . .
For the Lord's blessing rests upon
   every place one lets Her enter.

ECCLESIASTICUS

My son, If you find a man who knows Sophia,
rise early to visit him,
and let your feet wear out his doorstep.

Listen, my son, accept my judgment;
do not reject my advice:
Put your feet in Sophia's fetters
and your neck in Her collar.
Stoop to carry Her on your shoulders
and do not chafe at Her bonds.
Come to Her whole-heartedly,
and keep to Her ways with all your might.
Follow Her track, and She will make Herself known to you;
And once you have grasped Her, never let Her go.
In the end She will transform Herself into pure joy;
Her fetters will become your strong defense
and Her collar a gorgeous robe.

STOIC PHILOSOPHERS

—

MARCUS AURELIUS
EPICTETUS
SENECA

υδὲ τοῖς τυχοῦσιν
ληπτα εἶναι· πλὴν
ὑσκατάληπτα δοκεῖ·
:ατάθεσις μεταπτωτ:
ιέτιθι τοίνυν ἐπ' αὐτ(
(ρονα καὶ εὐτελῆ
:ιναίδου ἢ πόρνης ἢ
πιθι ἐπὶ τὰ τῶν σ
στὶ καὶ τοῦ χαριεσ
.έγω, ὅτι καὶ ἑαυτόν
 Ἐν τοιούτῳ οὖν ζ(
ύσει τῆς τε οὐσίας
ινήσεως καὶ τῶν
ὸ ἐκτιμηθῆναι ἢ
υνάμενον, οὐδ' ἐπι(
·αραμυθούμενον ἑαυτ
.ύσιν, καὶ μὴ ἀσχα
ούτοις μόνοις προσ(
τι οὐδὲν συμβήσετ(
ῶν ὅλων φύσιν ἐστί

Stoicism began in 310 B.C. and gets its name from *Stoa,* meaning "the porch," the place in Athens where its founder, Zeno, gave his discourses. Zeno's aim was to disseminate the teachings of the great philosophers—Plato, Aristotle, Pythagoras, and Heraclitus—which for so long had been the sole property of the learned class.

The Stoics viewed God as the living universe, as the Supreme Intelligence that held everything in order; and they saw a spark of this divine power in everyone. Although the Stoics insisted that there was only one supreme power, they saw it as having many aspects and referred to each by a different name—Nature, Providence, Law, Wisdom, Destiny, Zeus.

The most famous Stoic was **Marcus Aurelius** (A.D. 121–180), the last of the great Roman emperors. A small journal he kept toward the end of his life, which is now titled *The Meditations,* has done more to make Stoicism known to the world than any other work. Paradoxically, Marcus was not a true Stoic, for the true Stoic was steadfast, unflinching, and indifferent to the pains and pleasures of life. Marcus, however, was endearingly mortal; he struggled with life. His *Meditations* are not written with staunch certainty, but with the thoughtful words of one still searching. His writing is filled with such intimacy and sincerity that we no longer feel in the company of a Roman emperor but of an old and reliable friend.

In the Piazza Campidoglia in Rome stands a statue of Marcus Aurelius of which Henry James once wrote, "In the capital of Christendom, the portrait most suggestive of a Christian conscience is that of a pagan emperor."

Another noble Stoic was **Lucius Annaeus Seneca** (4 B.C.–A.D. 65), a brilliant Roman statesman and tragic playwright whose work influenced much of Elizabethan drama. He was a staunch humanitarian, calling hatred "the most dangerous, outrageous, brutal, and intractable of all passions." It can readily be seen why his ideas and writings were embraced by Martin Luther King, Jr., and other leaders of the American civil rights movement of the 1960s.

Epictetus (A.D. 1st century) was born in Greece yet spent most of his life as a Roman slave. Whereas Marcus Aurelius wrote about Nature and the Supreme Intelligence, and Seneca about social issues, Epictetus—bearing the mark of his difficult life—stressed complete dispassion toward outer circumstances and the need to find happiness within oneself. His one volume of writings is called, *The Golden Sayings of Epictetus*.

Marcus Aurelius

At daybreak, when you loathe the idea of leaving your bed, have this thought ready in your mind: "I am rising for the work of man." Should I have misgivings about doing that for which I was born, and for the sake of which I came into this world? Is this the grand purpose of my existence: to lie here snug and warm underneath my blankets?—"Certainly it feels more pleasant."—Was it for pleasure that you were made, and not for work, nor for effort? Look at the plants, sparrows, ants, spiders, and bees, all working busily away, each doing its part in welding an orderly Universe. So who are you to go against the bidding of Nature? Who are you to refuse man his share of the work?

To live each day as though it were your last—never flustered, never lazy, never a false word—herein lies the perfection of character.

Marcus Aurelius

Think of all the years passed by in which you said to yourself "I'll do it tomorrow," and how the gods have again and again granted you periods of grace of which you have not availed yourself. It is time to realize that you are a member of the Universe, that you are born of Nature itself, and to know that a limit has been set to your time. Use every moment wisely, to perceive your inner refulgence, or 'twill be gone and nevermore within your reach.

In a man's life, his time is but a moment, his being a mere flux, his senses a dim glimpse, his body food for the worms, and his soul a restless eddy . . . the things of the body pass like a flowing stream; life is a brief sojourn; and one's mark in this world is soon forgotten.

Marcus Aurelius

Constantly remind yourself, "I am a member of the whole body of conscious things." If you think of yourself as a mere "part," then love for mankind will not well up in your heart; you will look for some reward in every act of kindness and miss the boon which the act itself is offering. Then all your work will be seen as a mere duty and not as the very porthole connecting you with the Universe itself.

Men may block your path, but never let them obstruct you from right action; never let them destroy the feeling of charity you have toward them. You must be firm in both: steadfast in judgment and action; kind to those who do you harm. To lose your temper with them is no less a sign of weakness than one cowed into abandoning his proper course of action. In both cases, the post of duty has been deserted.

As Marcus, I have Rome; as a human being, I have the Universe. What brings benefit to these communities, that alone is what brings benefit to me.

MARCUS AURELIUS

Is your cucumber bitter?—throw it away. Are there briars in your path?—turn aside. That is enough. Do not dwell on the thought, "Why have such things been brought into the world?" A man of true wisdom would only laugh at you, just as a carpenter would laugh at you if you found fault with the shavings lying about his shop. The carpenter, at least, has a place to throw out his scraps; yet Nature has no such place outside Herself. And this is the miracle of Her workmanship: though limited to Herself, She takes back everything that is old, worn out, and useless; and from within Herself, brings forth a new creation. She requires neither a substance outside Herself, nor a place to discard the waste: Her own space, Her own material, and Her own workmanship is sufficient unto Her.

MARCUS AURELIUS

There is one type of person who, whenever he does a kind deed, will not hesitate to ask for some reward. Another type of person, though not so bold, will keep track of everything he has done for you, feeling deep down that you are in his debt. Then there are those who give without any remembrance of what they have done. They are like the vine that has brought forth a cluster of grapes, and having once borne its delicious fruit, seeks nothing more. As the horse that runs its race, the hound that tracks its game, and the bee that hives its honey, so should a man be when he has done an act of kindness: not seeking reward, not proclaiming his virtues, but passing on to the next act, as the vine passes on to bear another cluster of summer grapes.

Life is the way you see it.

Marcus Aurelius

It is said:
"Face the stormy winds that blow from God
With steady oars and uncomplaining hearts."

It is possible to live out your whole life in perfect content-ment, even though the whole world deafens you with its roar and wild beasts tear apart your body like a lump of clay. For nothing can shake a steady mind out of its peaceful repose; nothing can bar it from correct judgment, or defeat its readi-ness to see the benefit that all things bring. True understand-ing is to see the events of life in this way: "You are here only for my benefit, though rumor paints you otherwise." And everything is turned to one's advantage when he greets a situation like this: "You are the very thing I was looking for." Truly, whatever arises in life is the right material to bring about your growth and the growth of those around you. This, in a word, is *art*—and this art called "life" is a practice suitable to both men and gods. Everything contains some special purpose and a hidden blessing; what then could be strange or arduous, when all of life is here to greet you like an old and faithful friend?

Love that which is woven for you in the pattern of your destiny. What could be better suited for your growth?

Marcus Aurelius

Remember, it is the Hidden Power within us that pulls the strings; there lies the guiding force, there is the life, there, one might say, is the man himself. Never think of yourself as a mere body with its various appendages. The body is like the axe of a carpenter: dare we think the axe to be the carpenter himself? Without this Inner Cause, which dictates both action and inaction, the body is of no more use than the weaver's shuttle without a weaver, the writer's pen without a writer, or the coachman's whip without a horse and carriage.

Honor the highest thing in the Universe; it is the power on which all things depend; it is the light by which all of life is guided. Honor the highest within yourself; for it too is the power on which all things depend, and the light by which all life is guided.

Dig within. Within is the wellspring of Good; and it is always ready to bubble up, if you just dig.

Marcus Aurelius

You have seen a hand, a foot, or perhaps a head severed from its body and lying some distance away. Such is the state a man brings himself to—as far as he is able—when he refuses to accept what befalls him, breaks away from helping others, or pursues self-seeking action. You become an outcast from the unity of Nature; though born of it, your own hand has cut you from it. Yet here is the beautiful proviso: it lies within your own power to join Nature once again. God has not granted such favor to any other part of creation: to return again, after having been separated and cleft asunder.

O Universe, all that is in tune with you is also in tune with me! Every note of your harmony resonates in my innermost being. For me nothing is early and nothing is late, if it is timely for you. O Nature, all that your seasons bring is fruit for me. From thee come all things; in thee do all things live and grow; and to thee do all things return. "Dear City of God" is our cry, even though the poets say, "Dear City of Cecrops."

Waste no more time talking about great souls and how they should be. Become one yourself!

EPICTETUS

Show me a Stoic.
Show me a man modelled after the doctrines
    that are ever upon his lips.
Show me a man who is hard-pressed,
    and happy,
In danger, and happy,
On his death-bed—and happy,
In exile—and happy,
In evil report—and happy.

Show him to me.
I ask again.

So help me Heaven,
    I long to see *one* Stoic!
And if you cannot show me one fully realized,
    let me at least see one in whom the process is at work—
    one whose bent is in that direction.
Do me that favor!
Grudge it not to an old man
    to behold a sight of such wonder.
Do you think I wish to see the *Zeus* or *Athena* of Phidias,
    sparkling with ivory and gold?—
No. Show me one of you,
    a human soul,
        longing to be one with God.

EPICTETUS

The Philosophers would have us first learn that there is a God, and that His Will directs the Universe. . . . Secondly, what the nature of God is. Whatever that nature is discovered to be, the man who would please and obey Him must strive with all his might to be made like unto Him. If the Divine is faithful, he also must be faithful; if free, he also must be free; if beneficent, he also must be beneficent; if magnanimous, he also must be magnanimous. Thus as an imitator of God, he must follow Him in every thought, word and deed.

EPICTETUS

If we had understanding,
Would we ever cease chanting and blessing
    the Divine Power,
Both openly and in secret?
Whether digging or ploughing or eating,
    should we not sing a hymn to God?—

Great is God,
    for He has given us the instruments
    to till the ground . . .
He has given us hands,
    the power of digestion,
    and the wisdom of the body which controls the breath.

Great is God,
    for he has given us a mind
    and the power of discrimination.

What else can I that am old and lame do
    but sing to God?
Were I a nightingale,
    I should do after the manner of a nightingale.
Were I a swan,
    I should do after the manner of a swan.
But now, since I am a reasonable man,
    I must sing to God.
This is my work.

I will do it;
  I will not desert my post.

And I call upon you too, to join in this self-same hymn.

SENECA

To see a man fearless in danger,
Untainted by lust,
Happy in adversity,
Composed in turmoil,
And laughing at all those things
    which are either coveted or feared by others—
All men must acknowledge,
    that this can be nothing else but a beam of divinity
    animating a human body.

SENECA

What is God?—
    The Mind of the universe.
What is He?—
    All that you see, and all that you don't see.

Guide and guardian of the universe;
Soul and spirit of the world;
Builder and master of so great a work—
    to Him all names belong.
Would you call Him *Destiny*?
    You will not err:
Cause of causes, on Him all depends.
Had you rather say *Providence*?
    This will be right:
By His plan the world is watched over
    insuring that it goes safely through its motions.
Or *Nature*?
    This title does Him no wrong:
Of Him all things are born, and in Him all things live.
Or *Universe*?
    You are not mistaken:
He is all that we see,
    wholly present in every part,
    sustaining this entire creation.

SENECA

Hatred is not only a vice,
   but a vice which goes point-blank against Nature;
For it divides instead of joining,
   and frustrates the end of God's will in human society.
One man was born to help another;
Hatred makes us destroy one another.
Love unites,
   hatred separates;
Love is beneficial,
   hatred is destructive.
Love succors even strangers,
   hatred destroys the most intimate friendship;
Love fills all hearts with joy,
   hatred ruins all those who possess it.
Nature is bountiful, but hatred is pernicious;
For it is not hatred, but mutual love,
   that holds all mankind together.

SUFI POETS

~

JALALUDDIN RUMI
JAMI
GHALIB
NAZIR
FAKHRUDDIN ARAQI
IBN AL ARABI
MAHMUD SHABISTARI
FIRDAUSI

Sufism is a mystical sect of Islam based on love, devotion, and the ever-present longing to merge with God, the Beloved. *Islam* means "submission," and in this regard the Sufis are true pillars of Islam: although they ignore the traditional Muslim practices and rituals, they submit themselves with complete abandon to the call of Divine Love.

The Sufis are famed for their simple lifestyle, their ecstatic whirling, their illumined poetry, and their insistence on the need for direct experience of Love in the Heart. Like many religious sects, the Sufis developed a secret language to describe their divine intoxication, with the most distinct metaphors revolving around taverns, wine, and drunkenness. This symbolism is especially powerful, and highlights the other-worldly quality of the Sufi experience, because wine is forbidden in Islam, yet promised in Paradise.

The most famous Sufi was **Jalaluddin Rumi** (1207–1273) whose writings are filled with spiritual gems and whose exquisite work, the *Mathnawi,* is called "the Koran of Persia." The first part of Rumi's life was spent as a scholar until he met a wandering dervish named Shams-i Tabriz. Many legends surround this meeting, yet all tell of the dramatic destruction of Rumi's books, and his realization that book knowledge is useless. Rumi's son wrote, "After meeting Shams, my father danced all day and sang all night. He had been a scholar—he became a poet; he had been an ascetic—he became drunk with love." From then on, all of Rumi's life was a consecration of this meeting with Shams; and his every word a testament of Divine Love for his Master.

Ibn al Arabi (1165–1240) was a Muslim born in Murcia, Spain. Although not Persian, his *Meccan Revelations,* and philosophy of *Unity*, established him as the greatest mystic of Islam. The philosophy of *Unity* holds that there is no real difference between the Essence and its attributes or, put another way, between God and the universe.

Fahkruddin Araqi (1213–1289) was a distinguished Master, who, in fits of ecstasy, would reel off line after line of inspired verse to his disciples. His one masterpiece, *Lama'at (Divine Flashes),* captures the essence of Sufi thought.

Two Persian poets of lasting influence were *Jami* (1414–1492), and *Mahmud Shabistari* (?1250–?1320). Jami was famed in his day as a court poet and mystic leader; he also kept correspondence with many Islamic rulers including Sultan Mohammed II, the conqueror of Constantinople. Today he is considered one of the most remarkable geniuses Persia ever produced. Shabistari's only work, *Gulshan i Raz (The Garden of Secrets),* is revered by all as a masterpiece of Sufi literature.

Ghalib (1797–1869) was a leading mystic of Rumi's school in Istanbul and famed for his Urdu poetry. *Nazir* (1735–1846) was a singing minstrel who filled the back streets of Delhi with the sound of his guitar and the sweet longing of his voice. He was humble and simple and was regarded as the great poet of the poor. *Firdausi* (?940–?1020) was a poet from Khurasan (northwest Iran) whose magnum opus, the *Shah-nameh,* is an epic poem of 60,000 rhyming couplets.

Jalaluddin Rumi

Come, come, whoever you are,
Wanderer, worshipper, lover of leaving,
    it doesn't matter.
Ours is a caravan of endless joy.
Even if you've broken your vows a hundred times—
Come, come, yet again come!

JALALUDDIN RUMI

The Lover is ever drunk with love;
　　He is free,
　　He is mad,
He dances with ecstasy and delight.
Caught by our own thoughts,
　　we worry about every little thing,
But once we get drunk on that love,
Whatever will be, will be.

When *you* dance,
　　the whole universe dances.
What wonder!
I've looked,
　　and now I cannot look away.
Take me, or do not take me,
　　both are the same,
As long as there is life in this body,
　　I am here to serve you.

Love came and it made me empty.
Love came and it filled me with the Beloved.
　　It became the blood in my veins,
　　It became my arms and my legs.
　　It became everything!
Now all I have is a name,
　　the rest belongs to the Beloved.

JALALUDDIN RUMI

I see His face,
I see His smile,
 There is my joy!
I feel His anger
I feel His heavy hand.
 There is my joy!
But what is this?—
 He has asked for my head!
My head does not matter—
He has asked me for something,
 There is my joy!

My eyes see only the face of the Beloved.
What a glorious sight,
 for that sight is beloved.
Why speak of two?
The Beloved is in the sight,
 and the sight is in the Beloved.

There is a force within that gives you life—
 Seek that.
In your body there lies a priceless jewel—
 Seek that.
Oh, wandering Sufi,
 if you are in search of the greatest treasure,
 don't look outside,
Look within, and seek That.

Jalaluddin Rumi

Our drunkenness does not come from wine,
Our gathering, so full of cheer,
    does not come from song or dance.
Without a pretty girl to fill our cup,
Without friend, without music, without wine,
We burst out like madmen,
    rolling drunk on the floor.

Don't think.
Don't get lost in your thoughts.
Your thoughts are a veil on the face of the Moon.
That Moon is your heart,
    and those thoughts cover your heart.
So let them go,
    just let them fall into the water.

If you want great wealth,
    and that which lasts forever,
Wake up!
If you want to shine
    with the love of the Beloved,
Wake up!
You've slept a hundred nights,
    And what has it brought you?
For your Self, for your God,
Wake up! Wake up!
Sleep no more.

JALALUDDIN RUMI

In one sweet moment she burst out from my heart,
And there she sat before me
    drinking ruby-red wine.
Trapped by her beauty
    I saw and I touched—
My whole face became eyes,
My every eye became hands.

I cried, and I burned in that cry.
I kept silent, and I burned in that silence.
Then I stayed away from extremes—
    I went right down the middle,
And I burned in that middle.

It is said,
    "God's Light shines in all six directions."
A shout came from the crowd:
    "So where is that Light?"
    "Shall I fix my gaze to the left,
    or to the right?"
It is said,
    "For a moment, fix it neither to the left
    nor to the right."

JALALUDDIN RUMI

I know nothing of two worlds,
  all I know is the One.
I seek only One,
I know only One,
I find only One,
  and I sing of only One.
I am so drunk with the wine of the Beloved
  that both worlds have slipped from my reach.
Now I have no business here,
  Save to reach for the cup of my Beloved.

Oh, I'm alive,
But this pain is worse than death.
My heart pounds, my body shakes,
  my stomach burns with pangs of hunger.
At least with hunger
  the more you eat, the less it gets,
But not with this,
  for the more I eat, the worse it gets.

Oh my soul,
I searched the whole world,
  but could not find you anywhere.
All I found was my Beloved.
Call me cruel,
Call me blind,
Call me anything, I don't mind,
Oh my soul,
  I call you *my Beloved.*

JALALUDDIN RUMI

The smile on your face is sight enough.
The sound of your name is song enough.
Why cut me down with your deadly arrows,
    When the shadow of your whip is reason enough?

O my Beloved!
Take me,
Liberate my soul,
Fill me with your love,
    and release me from both worlds.
When I set my heart on anything but you
    a fire burns me from inside.
O my Beloved!
Take away what I want,
Take away what I do,
Take away everything,
    that takes me from you.

Some say, "Love combined with wisdom is the best."
Others say, "Discipline and regular practice is the best."
O, these words are more precious than gold—
But my life offered to Shams-i Tabriz is the best.

Jalaluddin Rumi

All through time that same Beauty
  has risen in a different shape,
  beckoned the soul, and disappeared.
Every moment that Loved One
  puts on a new garment—
  now of old, now of new.
Entering the heart of the world
  like potter's clay,
  the Spirit plunges in like a diver,
Then rises up from the mud,
  molded and baked.

He appeared as Noah, and safely entered the Ark
  when a deluge swept over the world.
He became Abraham,
  and walked through the midst of fire,
  which turned into roses for His sake.
For a while He roamed the earth, unknown,
  helping those in need.
Then He became Jesus,
  and ascended to the dome of heaven
  in glory of God.
In all, it was He
  who came and went in every generation.
Then He appeared in the form of the Prophet,
  and gained the empire of Islam.

What essence is preserved?
What moves from one reality to the next?

The lovely winner of hearts became a sword
    and appeared in the hand of Ali,
    the slayer of time.
When Mansur yelled out, "I am the Truth"
    they hanged him as a heretic.
But no! No! It was *He* that cried out,
    "I am the Truth."
It was *He* that mounted the scaffold.

Rumi has spoken the truth.
But no! Do not listen to Rumi—
    It is *He* that speaks the truth.

JAMI

All through eternity
    Beauty unveils His exquisite form
    in the solitude of nothingness;
He holds a mirror to His Face
    and beholds His own beauty.
He is the knower and the known,
    the seer and the seen;
No eye but His own
    has ever looked upon this Universe.

His every quality finds an expression:
Eternity becomes the verdant fields of Time and Space;
Love, the life-giving garden of this world.
Every branch and leaf and fruit
Reveals an aspect of His perfection—
    The cypress gives hint of His majesty,
    The rose gives tidings of His beauty.

Wherever Beauty looks,
    Love is also there;
Wherever Beauty shows a rosy cheek
    Love lights Her fire from that flame.
When Beauty dwells in the dark folds of night
    Love comes and finds a heart
    entangled in her tresses.
Beauty and Love are as body and soul.
Beauty is the mine, Love is the diamond.

They have been together
    since the beginning of time—
Side by side, step by step.

GHALIB

I leave with scars
    and the ache of longings still unmet.
I am a candle,
        blown naked in the wind,
        not fit to stand at the table
        where men rejoice.

Everyone! Come!
Our door is open, our vision is clear.
Here we see only what is true—
"The high, the low, the good, the bad,"
    we can see none of this.

My yearning has loosened
    the veil hiding Beauty.
She is now mine—but alas,
    My own sight is there
    blocking the view.

The beat of my own heart
    sounds in my ear.
The wish to live as others do
    has long been silenced.
What does their world have to offer?—
Nothing but the echo of voices
    yelling, "more, more."

"I do not fear love's cruelty."
But my friend, your heart
    which beats so proudly
    is the first thing She will take.

GHALIB

This world is nothing more than
    Beauty's chance to show Herself.
And what are we?—
Nothing more than Beauty's chance to see Herself.
For if Beauty were not seeking Herself
    we would not exist.

Every particle of creation
    sings its own song
    of what is, and what is not.
The wise hear what is;
The mad hear what is not.
And only a cracked mirror
    will show a difference.

All your knowledge
    leads you in the wrong direction;
All your worship
    only puts you to sleep.
Insipid is this world
    which only believes in what is seen;
Here, taste the wine from this Cup
    which cannot be seen.

The one who has adorned himself
    with the Creator's form
Is the only one fit to guard
    the purity
    of both worlds.

On account of those who repeat His Name,
This Earth has become a paradise,
   an honored place
    in the order of creation.
God's love is on this Earth,
And the heavens
   forever bend over to greet Her.

NAZIR

My dear friend.
How am I to tell of the many vagaries
    on the path of love?
How am I to speak of what happened to me?

All of a sudden
    tears began to flow from my eyes,
And I was filled with a desire
    to find the one
    whom everyone adores.

All poise and decorum left me
    as the yearning to meet Him
    rose up from within my heart.
I became impatient, restless,
    unmindful of my actions.

I soon dyed my garments in red,
    and put a garland around my neck.
I rubbed ashes on my body,
    adorned myself with a string of beads,
    and became a yogi to all who saw me.
Thus attired, I began my quest.

As a yogi
    I looked for my Beloved
    from door to door;
In the lanes and in the streets
I searched for Him.

My heart was burning with fire.
Sometimes I howled like a madman,
Other times I cried like a babe.
Sighs from my lips came out as hot vapor;
A flood of tears fell from my eyes,
    and all the world spun round me.
My madness drew a crowd.
I sought my Friend in flesh and blood,
    but all I ever got were excuses.

Whoever came before me I asked,
    "O tell me, where can I meet my Beloved?"

Sometimes I took to a rosary;
With every bead that passed through my fingers I asked,
    "Where is He? Where is He?"

I knew nothing;
    I knew not what to seek,
    I knew not where to go.
Whom was I to ask and where was I to wander?
What path to follow?
What instructions to pursue,
    whereby I might find my Beloved?

Seeking Him I reached the mosque.
But all I found there were vain discussions
    on sacraments and ceremonials.

My heart told me to go to a seminary;
Maybe there I might meet my Lord.
But all I met was the uproar of discussion,
    the scholars puffed with their eloquence.

I was advised to go visit the temple.
There I found
    only idols being worshipped
    and gongs being sounded.
Disgusted, I sought a stone
    to strike my head against;
For nowhere could I find
    that callous Beloved of mine.

Then I went on a pilgrimage
    to all the holy spots.
Maybe I would find my Beloved there.
So I stopped at every holy place
    and bowed before many blessed deities,
But it brought me no comfort.
And when I found myself helpless,
    I left the towns and their temples
    to wander in the jungle.

In the wilderness I wept and shed hot tears.
I asked myself, how long must I bear this agony
    of separation?
But there was nowhere to go,
    no place to find shelter from my pain.

For days I roamed in the forest,
    a poor man, a pilgrim, a homeless fakir.
In the mountains too, I struggled:
Empty, hungry, thirsty—in a miserable plight,
    without a morsel to appease my hunger,
    without a drop to quench my thirst.

One day I was lying in a field,
    the burning sun overhead.

My mind was filled with the desire to see Him.
But all was in vain:
The Lord would not
    show Himself to me.
I shed tears of blood
    that sparkled like rubies in the sands.

When I reached a state of total despair,
    hoping that death might rescue me from this pain,
    He, my careless Beloved,
Came to me.
Like a mother rushing to her sick child,
He came to me,
    sat by my side,
    and placed my head upon His lap.
Kind words flowed from His lips:

"Now see whatever you want to see,
I will reveal to you all the secrets of my heart.
Remember, first we test our lover;
    torture him, oppress him,
    and force him to shed tears.
Then we invite him to us.
When all his thoughts are of the Beloved,
We allow him to come near,
    shower him with grace,
    and hold him in our arms.
Thus he becomes perfect."

As these words reached my ears
I came back to life, gained consciousness,
    and was freed of all pain.
Then, I cast one look
    at His radiant face

And the mystery of all creation
    lay bare before me.
In one moment
    the good and bad actions of lifetimes
    vanished.

From separation I passed into Unity;
All the illusions of life disappeared
    like a phantom show.
Now wherever I cast my glance,
I see Him alone, and none other.
The Muslim, the Hindu, and the Jew
Have all become the same to me—
    they have all merged in the
Glory of my one Beloved.

So says Nazir.

FAKHRUDDIN ARAQI

I look into the mirror and see my own beauty;
I see the Truth of the universe revealing itself as me.

I rise in the sky as the morning Sun, do not be surprised,
Every particle of creation is me alone.

What are the holy spirits? my essence revealed.
And the human body? the vessel of my own form.

What is the ocean that encircles the world?
A drop of my abundant Grace;
And the purest light that fills every soul?
A spark of my own illumination.

I am Light itself, reflected in the heart of everyone;
I am the treasure of the Divine Name,
    the shining Essence of all things.

I am every light that shines,
Every ray that illumines the world.

From the highest heavens to the bedrock of the earth
All is but a shadow of my splendor.

If I dropped the veil covering my true essence
The world would be gone—lost in a brilliant light.

What is the water that gives eternal life?
A drop of my divine nectar.
And the breath that brings the dead back to life?
A puff of my breath, the breath of all life . . .

Fakhruddin Araqi

Every word of every tongue is
    Love telling a story to her own ears.

Every thought in every mind,
    She whispers a secret to her own Self.

Every vision in every eye,
    She shows her beauty to her own sight.

Every smile on every face,
    She reveals her own joy for herself to enjoy.

Love courses through everything,
No, Love *is* everything.
How can you say, *there is no love,*
    when nothing but Love exists?
All that you see has appeared because of Love.
    All shines from Love,
    All pulses with Love,
    All flows from Love—
No, once again, all *is* Love!

His Light rose,
    I found it in my own heart—
It is now my Light
    you see shining!

FAKHRUDDIN ARAQI

This world is nothing but a dance of shadows,
A line drawn between
    darkness and light,
    joy and oppression,
    time and eternity.
Learn to read this subtle line
    for it tells all the secrets of creation.

Although you may not know it,
If you love anyone, it is Him you love;
If you turn your head in any direction,
    it is toward Him you turn.

Let go of everything,
Completely lose yourself on this path,
Then your every doubt will be dispelled.
With absolute conviction you'll cry out—
I am God!
I am the one I have found!

In the light I praised you
    and never knew it.
In the dark I slept with you
    and never knew it.
I always thought that I was me,
But no, I was you
    and never knew it.

IBN AL ARABI

Listen, O Beloved!
I am the reality of the world, the center of the circle.
I am the parts and the whole.
I am the will holding Heaven and Earth in place.
And I have given you sight, only so you may see me.

O Beloved!
I call again and again, but you do not hear me,
I appear again and again, but you do not see me,
I fill myself with fragrance, again and again,
    but you do not smell me.
I become savory food, yet you do not taste me.
Why can't you reach me through your touch
Or breathe me in through sweet perfumes?
Love me,
Love yourself in me.
No one is deeper within you than I.
Others may love you for their sake,
But I love you for yourself.
    Dear Beloved!
    This bargain is not fair—
    If you approach me,
    It is only because I have approached you.

I am closer to you than yourself,
Than your soul, than your own breath.
Why do you not see me?
Why do you not hear me?
    I am so jealous—
I want you to see me, and no one else,

To hear me, and no one else,
    not even yourself.

Dear Beloved! Come with me.
Let us go to Paradise together.
And if we find any road
    that leads to separation,
We will destroy that road.
Let us go hand in hand
In the presence of the Truth;
Let it be our witness,
And let it seal forever
    this wondrous union of ours.

Mahmud Shabistari

"I" and "you" are the Pure Radiance,
Beams of one Light
 shining through the niches of a lamp.
Lift yourself above time and space
 and become time and space;
Leave behind this world
 and become a world unto yourself.

When "I" and "you" are bound by form
 a veil falls between us and our love.
Lift the veil
 and you will see the unity
 of all people.
Lift the veil and you will ask:
 What is mosque?
 What is synagogue?
 What is fire-temple?

Mahmud Shabistari

The eye is not strong enough
    to look at the brilliant sun;
But you can watch its light
    reflected in water.
Pure Being is too bright to behold,
    yet it can be seen
    reflected in the mirror of this world.
For Non-Being
    is set opposite of Being,
    and catches its image in every moment.

Every particle of the world is a mirror,
In each atom lies the blazing light
    of a thousand suns.
Cleave the heart of a rain-drop,
    a hundred pure oceans will flow forth.
Look closely at a grain of sand,
    the seed of a thousand beings can be seen.
The foot of an ant is larger than an elephant;
In essence, a drop of water
    is no different than the Nile.
In the heart of a barley-corn
    lies the fruit of a hundred harvests;
Within the pulp of a millet seed
    an entire universe can be found.
In the wing of a fly,
    an ocean of wonder;
In the pupil of the eye, an endless heaven.
Though the inner chamber of the heart is small,
    the Lord of both worlds
    gladly makes His home there.

Mahmud Shabistari

The tavern-haunter is a seeker of Unity,
    a soul freed from the shackles
    of himself.

The tavern is where lovers meet,
    the place where the bird of the soul takes rest.
It is a sanctuary that does not exist
    in a world that cannot be found.
The tavern-haunter wanders alone
    in a desolate place,
    seeing the whole world as a mirage.
The desert he walks through
    has no limit;
No one can reach its end.
You may wander there for a hundred years,
    and never see yourself or another.
Those who live there
    possess neither head nor feet,
    faith nor infidelity.
Drinking the wine of dispassion
    they have renounced good and evil alike;
Sipping from a cup of bliss,
    without lips or mouth,
They have cast away
All thoughts of name and fame,
All talk of marvels and visions,
All dreams of secret chambers and distant worlds.

They fall, and they rise again,
    between union and separation;
Now shedding tears of blood;

Now raised to a world of bliss,
    stretching their necks out like racers;
Now with blackened faces staring at a wall,
Or faces reddened by the wine of Unity.
Now in a mystic whirl,
    dancing in the arms of their Beloved,
    losing head and foot like the revolving heavens.
With every strain the minstrel plays,
    comes to them rapture of the unseen world;
With every note of this mystic ode
    a veil is torn from a priceless treasure.

Blind to this world,
Indifferent to great and small,
Ignorant of master and disciple,
They guzzle down cup after cup of wine,
    and still want more!
They sweep ancient dust from their souls.
They grab at their Beloved's clothes
    like a bunch of drunkards!
O Lord, who are these guys?—

    They are Sufis.

FIRDAUSI

If on earth there be
   a Paradise of Bliss,
It is this,
It is this,
It is this.

CHRISTIAN SAINTS

—

SAINT PAUL
THE PHILOKALIA
MEISTER ECKHART
RUSSIAN MONK
THOMAS À KEMPIS
JEAN PIERRE DE CAUSSADE

Christianity began as a sect of Judaism. At first their only difference was in the interpretation of the Messianic prophesies of the Hebrew Scriptures: Most Jews believed the Messiah was yet to come, the Nazarenes (as the earliest Christian sect was called) believed that Jesus *was* the Messiah. But with the increasing number of gentile converts and the acceptance of new ideas, Christianity evolved into a new religion of love and devotion, humility and faith, prayer, worship, and the adoration of Jesus Christ.

It is likely that Christianity would have remained a small Messianic cult had it not been for the efforts of **Saint Paul** (A.D. ?3–A.D. ?64). As a youth, Paul was one of the Jewish authorities who suppressed the Christian sect. All this changed while witnessing the stoning of a devout Christian: Paul was so struck by the martyr's unshakable faith and composure that he thought Jesus might be the Messiah. And the spiritual visions he had on the road to Damascus—dazzling lights, voices, sudden darkness—further convinced him that Jesus was the Messiah. The next thirty years of his life were spent travelling, teaching, and unifying the many newfound Christian groups. Through his dynamic leadership, the precepts of this new faith were shaped into a compelling and universal religion of salvation. Called "the second father of Christianity," Saint Paul is truly one of the few epochal figures in history.

One of the earliest works on the basic practice of Christianity is the **Philokalia** (A.D. 1st–4th century), a collection of writings by monks and abbots who applied Jesus's teachings to their own lives. Their most notable practice was the ceaseless Jesus Prayer—the continuous and uninterrupted calling on the name of Jesus with lips, mind, and soul; in every place, and at all times. Both the *Philokalia* and the Jesus Prayer were made famous in the West by an unknown **Russian Monk** (19th century) who tells of his spiritual adventures throughout Russia and the joy, happiness, and protection that come from ceaseless prayer.

The most influential Christian figure of the Middle Ages was the German preacher and theologian **Meister Eckhart** (1260–1329), whose ideas and writings—although officially condemned by the Catholic Church—were not only embraced by the great Christian mystics, such as Theresa of Avila and St. John of the Cross, but also marked the beginning of German philosophy and mysticism. With great intellectual power, and an "air of almost terrible certainty," he spoke about God, devotion, self-sacrifice, and the divine spark in man.

Shortly after Eckhart came a movement called *devotio moderna,* "the New Devotion," which called for complete surrender of selfhood and total devotion to God. This movement gave rise to the great mystic **Thomas à Kempis** (1380–1471), a monk and recluse, whose book *The Imitation of Christ* ranks second only to the Bible in its profound and lasting influence throughout Christendom. The New Devotion also echoed in the writings of the French priest **Jean Pierre de Caussade** (1675–1751), who saw the essence of Christianity, and all religious practice, as pivoting on but one thing: complete surrender to the Will of God. To him every moment and every event in life was sacred, because "God speaks to everyone through what is happening to them moment by moment."

Saint Paul

LOVE

Though I speak with the tongues of men and angels,
And have not love,
I am no better than a clanging gong
    or a brass bell.
And though I have the gift of prophesy,
    and know every hidden mystery;
    and though I have faith strong enough to move
    mountains,
And have not love,
    I am nothing.
And though I give away all I own to the poor,
    and offer my body to be burned,
And have not Love,
    I do not gain a thing.
Love is patient, Love is kind;
Love knows not jealousy,
Love is never boastful,
    nor proud, nor unseemly.
Love is not selfish nor easily provoked.
Love knows nothing of wrong,
    does not rejoice at the misfortune of others,
    and only delights in the Truth.
There is nothing Love cannot bear;
    no limit to its faith, its hope, or its endurance.
The reign of Love will never end.
But where there are prophesies, they will end;
Where there are tongues of ecstasy, they will end;
Where there is knowledge, it will end.

For our knowledge is only of a part,
    and our prophesies tell of but a part.
And that which is a part vanishes
    with the arrival of the whole.
When I was a child,
    I spoke as a child, I saw as a child,
    and I thought as a child.
When I grew up, I put away childish things.
Now we see everything through a murky glass,
    one day we will see God clearly,
    face to face.
Now my knowledge is incomplete,
    one day it will be perfect,
    like God's knowledge of me.
In a word,
    there are three things you are never to let go of:
Faith, hope, and love;
    but the greatest of these
    will always be love.

Saint Paul

THE APOSTLES

All of you, no doubt, have everything you could desire. You have come into your fortune already. You have come into your kingdom—and left us out. How I wish you had indeed won your kingdom; then you might share it with us! For it seems that God has made us apostles the most abject of mankind. We are like men condemned to death in the arena, a spectacle to the whole universe—angels as well as men. We are fools for Christ's sake, while you are so sensible Christians. We are weak; you are so powerful. We are in disgrace; you are honored. To this day we go hungry and thirsty and in rags; we are roughly handled; we wander from place to place; we wear ourselves out working with our hands. They curse us, and we bless; they persecute us, and we submit to it; they slander us, and we humbly make our appeal. . . .

As God's servants, we try to give ourselves in all circumstance by our steadfast endurance: in hardships and dire straits; flogged, imprisoned; overworked, sleepless, starving. We give ourselves by the innocence of our behavior, our grasp of truth, our patience and kindliness; by gifts of the Holy Spirit, by sincere love, by declaring the truth, by the power of God. . . . Honor and dishonor, praise and blame, are alike our lot; we are the imposters who speak the truth, the unknown men whom all men know; dying we still live on; disciplined by suffering, we are not done to death; in our sorrows we always have cause for joy; poor ourselves, we bring wealth to many; without a penny, we own the world.

Saint Paul

THE SPIRIT

There are a variety of gifts, but the same Spirit. There are varieties of service, but the same Lord. There are many forms of work, but all of them, in all men, are the work of the same God. In each of us the Spirit is manifested in one particular way, for some useful purpose. One man, through the Spirit, has the gift of wise speech, while another, by the power of the same Spirit, can put the deepest knowledge into words. Another, by the same Spirit, is granted faith; another, by the one Spirit, gifts of healing, and another miraculous powers; another has the gift of prophecy, and another the ability to distinguish true spirits from false; yet another the gift of ecstatic utterance of different kinds, and another the ability to interpret it. But all these gifts are the work of one and the same Spirit, distributing them separately, to each individual, at will.

Surely you know that you are God's temple, where the Spirit of God dwells. Anyone who destroys God's temple will himself be destroyed by God, because the temple of God is holy; and that temple is you.

THE PHILOKALIA

In creating man, God implanted in him something Divine —a certain thought, like a spark, having both light and warmth, a thought which illumines the mind and shows what is good and what is bad. This is called conscience and it is a natural law. By following this law the patriarchs and all the saints pleased God, even before the law was written. But when, through the fall, men covered up and trampled down conscience, there arose the need of written law, of holy Prophets, of the coming of our Lord Jesus Christ Himself, to uncover and raise it up, to rekindle this buried spark by the keeping of His holy commandments.

So let us guard our conscience, while we are in this world; let us not allow it to accuse us in something, nor disregard it in anything however small. For you must realize that from disregarding this small and insignificant thing we pass to neglect of big things.

If we were willing to make even small efforts, we would not suffer either much distress or difficulty. For if a man urges himself to make efforts, then, as he continues them, he gradually makes progress and later practices virtues with tranquility; for God, seeing him urge himself, sends him help. So let us urge ourselves, for, although we have not reached perfection, if we make efforts, through efforts we shall receive help, and with this help shall acquire all kinds of virtues. Therefore one of the fathers said, "Give blood and receive spirit," that is, strive earnestly and you will become perfect.

The wise Solomon says in the Proverbs, "They that have no guidance fall like leaves; but in much counsel there is safety." So you see what the Holy Scriptures teach us? They enjoin us not to rely on ourselves, not to regard ourselves as knowing all, not to believe that we can control ourselves, for we need help, and are in need of those who would counsel us according to God. No men are more unfortunate or nearer perdition than those who have no teachers of the way of God.

For what does it mean that where no guidance is, the people fall like leaves? A leaf is at first green, flourishing, beautiful; then it gradually withers, falls and is finally trampled underfoot. So it is with a man who has no guide: at first he is always zealous in fasting, vigil, silence, obedience, and other virtues; then his zeal, little by little, cools down and, having no one to instruct, support, and fire him up with zeal, he insensibly withers, falls, and finally becomes a slave of the enemies, who do with him what they will.

In every circumstance we must look upwards. Whether someone does good to us or we suffer harm from anyone, we must look upwards and thank God for all that befalls us.

THE PHILOKALIA

A soul pure in God is God.

One of perfect prayer is he who,
    withdrawing from all mankind,
    is united with all mankind.
One of perfect prayer is he who
    regards himself as existing with all people
    and sees himself in every person.

Blessed is he who regards every man
    as a god after God.
Blessed is he who looks on the salvation
    and progress of all as though it were his own.

MEISTER ECKHART

EMPTINESS

God must act when He finds you ready; for God cannot leave anything empty in man or in nature. Although you do not sense His presence, and feel totally empty of Him, I assure you it is not the case. For if there existed anything empty under heaven, either heaven would draw it up to itself, or bend down to fill it with itself. God, the Lord of all creation, must fill all that is empty.

I maintain by God's eternal truth that God must pour Himself, without reservation, with all His powers, into everyone who has sunk completely into himself and has touched bottom. For it is God's very nature to give Himself to all those who are empty. And God will give Himself so fully and completely that nothing will be left of Himself—nothing will be left of His essence, His nature, yea, His entire creation. God must pour *everything,* in its totality, into that person who has completely given himself to Him.

MEISTER ECKHART

On his way to church, a scholar was surprised to see a man in tattered clothes and barefoot. Nevertheless, as a good Christian, he greeted the poor man: "May God give you a good morning!"

The poor man replied cheerfully, "I have never yet had a bad morning."

"Then may God give you good luck!"

"I have never yet had bad luck."

"Well, may God give you happiness!"

"I have never yet been unhappy."

The scholar then asked the man, "Could you please explain yourself to me? I do not understand."

And the poor man replied, "With pleasure! You wish me a good morning, yet I have never had a bad morning. For when I am hungry, I praise God; when I feel cold, when it is raining or snowing, I praise God; and that is why I have never had a bad morning. You wish that God may give me luck, however, I have never had bad luck. This is because I live with God and always feel what he does is for the best. Whatever God sends me, be it pleasant or unpleasant, I accept with a grateful heart. That is why I have never had bad luck. Finally, you wish that God should make me happy. But I have never been unhappy. For all I desire is to follow God's will; I have surrendered my will so totally to God's will that, whatever God wants, that is what I also want. That is why I have never been unhappy."

MEISTER ECKHART

GOD'S WILL

A perfect and true will is one completely aligned with God's will and void of everything else. The more a man succeeds in following God's will, the more he joins in union with God: So if someone wished to touch him, he would first have to touch God; if someone wanted to approach him, he would first have to pass through God. By aligning itself with God's will, the soul takes on the taste of God: grief and joy, bitterness and sweetness, darkness and light—all become divine, whatever happens to this man.

Not one is so unprepared, unlearned, or uncouth that he could not become one with God. If he is ready to unite his will purely and unreservedly with the will of God, all he has to do is say, "Lord show me thy will and grant me the strength to fulfill it!" And God does so with abundance.

That we may follow God, that our will may become one with His—may God help us!

MEISTER ECKHART

THE KINGDOM OF GOD

Come now, noble souls, and take a look at the splendor you are carrying within yourselves! But if you do not let go of yourself completely, if you do not drown yourself in this bottomless sea of the Godhead, you cannot get to know this divine light.

When the soul is totally lost, it finds that it is the very self which it sought for so long in vain. Here the soul *is* God. Here it enjoys supreme bliss; here it is sufficient unto itself; here it shines with its own radiance. Here at last it has found that the Kingdom of God is itself!

You need not look for God either here or there. He is no farther away than the door of your heart: there He stands waiting till He finds you ready to open the door and let Him enter. No need for you to call Him from afar. He is waiting more impatiently than you for the door to be opened. He wants you a thousand times more urgently than you want Him. There is only one thing you must do: open and enter.

No one has ever longed so much for anything as God is longing to bring man to Him. God is so close to us, but we are distant and turned away from Him. God is within, we are without; God is at home with us, we are strangers to ourselves.

MEISTER ECKHART

DIVINE BIRTH

Never has anything become so kindred, so alike, so one with another, as the soul becomes with God in this birth. . . . In this birth, God flows into the soul with such a dazzling light that God and the soul become inexplicitly merged into one—one spirit, one essence, one Being.

God has given birth to the Son as you, as me, as each one of us. As many beings—as many gods in God.

In my soul, God not only gives birth to me as His son, He gives birth to me as *Himself,* and Himself as me.

My physical father is my father with but a small part of his being, and I am separate from him. He may be dead, and I may live. God, however, is my father with His entire being, because I am always His; I am alive only because He is alive.

In this divine birth I find that God and I are the same: I am what I was and what I shall remain, now and forever. I am carried above the highest angels; I neither decrease nor increase, for in this birth I have become the motionless cause of all that moves. I have won back what has always been mine. Here, in my own soul, the greatest of all miracles has taken place—God has returned to God!

Russian Monk

By the grace of God I am a Christian man . . . and by calling a homeless wanderer of the humblest birth who roams from place to place. My worldly goods are a knapsack with some dried bread in it on my back, and in my breast-pocket a Bible. And that is all.

A Christian is bound to perform many good works, but before all else what he ought to do is pray, for without prayer no other good work whatever can be accomplished. Without prayer he cannot find the way to the Lord, he cannot understand the truth, he cannot crucify the flesh with its passions and lusts, his heart cannot be enlightened with the light of Christ, he cannot be savingly united to God. None of those things can be effected unless they are preceded by constant prayer.

RUSSIAN MONK

When I prayed with my heart, everything around me seemed delightful and marvelous. The trees, the grass, the birds, the earth, the air, the light seemed to be telling me that they existed for man's sake, that they witnessed to the love of God for man, that everything proved the love of God for man, that all things prayed to God and sang His praise.

Sometimes my understanding, which had been so stupid before, was given so much light that I could easily grasp and dwell upon matters of which up to now I had not been able even to think at all. Sometimes that sense of a warm gladness in my heart spread throughout my whole being and I was deeply moved as the fact of the presence of God everywhere was brought home to me. Sometimes by calling upon the name of Jesus I was overwhelmed with bliss, and now I knew the meaning of the words *The Kingdom of God is within you.*

The Prayer of my heart gave me such consolation that I felt there was no happier person on earth than I, and I doubted if there could be greater and fuller happiness in the kingdom of Heaven. Not only did I feel this in my own soul, but the whole outside world also seemed to me full of charm and delight. Everything drew me to love and thank God: people, trees, plants, animals. I saw them all as my kinsfolk, I found in all of them the magic of the Name of Jesus. Sometimes I felt as light as though I had no body and was floating happily through the air instead of walking. Sometimes when I withdrew into myself I saw clearly all my internal organs, and I was filled with wonder at the wisdom with which the human body is made. . . . And at all such times of happiness, I wished that God would . . . let me pour out my heart in thankfulness at His feet.

Thomas à Kempis

LOVE

O my Lord God, most faithful Lover, when You come into my heart, all within me rejoices. You are my glory and the joy of my soul, my hope and my whole refuge in all my troubles.

Love is a great and good thing; it alone makes burdens light and bears in equal balance things pleasing and displeasing. Love endures every hardship and does not feel it, and love makes bitter things tasteful and sweet. The noble love of Jesus perfectly imprinted in man's soul makes him do great things, and stirs him always to desire perfection.

Nothing is sweeter than love; nothing higher, nothing stronger, nothing larger, nothing more joyful, nothing fuller, nothing better, in heaven or on earth; for love descends from God, and may not finally rest in anything lower than God. One with such love flies high; he runs swiftly, he is merry in God, he is free in soul. He gives all for all, and has all in all, for he rests in one high Goodness above all things, from whom all goodness flows.

Thomas à Kempis

LOVE

Love wakes much and sleeps little and, even in sleeping, does not sleep. It faints yet is not weary; it is restricted in its liberty yet is in great freedom. It sees reason to fear, yet does not fear, but, like an ember or a spark of fire, flames always upward, by the fervor of its love, toward God, and through the special help of grace is delivered from all perils and dangers.

He who is thus a spiritual lover knows well what that voice means which says: You, Lord God, are my whole love and desire. You are all mine, and I all Yours. Dissolve my heart into Your love so that I may know how sweet it is to serve You and how joyful it is to praise You, and to be as though I were all melded into Your love. Oh, I am urged on by love and go far above myself because of the great fervor I feel through Your unspeakable goodness. I shall sing to You the song of love; I shall follow You, my Beloved, in flights of thought wherever You go, and my soul will never be weary in praising You with the joyful songs of unconditional love.

Jean Pierre de Caussade

Come, all you simple souls;
    souls without devotion, grand talents,
    or lessons learned.

Come, you,
    who understand nothing of spiritual terms,
    who are filled with amazement
        at the eloquence of the learned.
Come, and I will teach you a secret,
    unreachable by those brilliant scholars—
The secret of perfection.
You will find this perfection within you,
    above you,
    below you,
    with every step you take.
Then you will be united with God—
    hand in hand you will walk.

Come, not to study the map of spiritual terrain,
But to possess it for yourself;
    To walk about in it
    without fear of going astray.

Why learn the theory of Divine Grace,
    and what it has been doing throughout history,
    when you can become the very instrument
    of its operation?

Come, not to discuss
    the words of others,
But to listen . . .

For in the sacredness of every moment
Divine Grace is telling to you alone
all that is required.

Jean Pierre de Caussade

ABANDONMENT

The essence of all spirituality is contained in this phrase: "complete and utter abandonment to the will of God."

We must offer ourselves to God like a clean, smooth canvas and not worry ourselves about what God may choose to paint on it, but at each moment, feel only the stroke of His brush. . . . It is the same with a piece of stone. Each blow from the sculptor's chisel makes it feel—if it could— as if it were being destroyed. As blow after blow descends, the stone knows nothing of how the sculptor is shaping it. All it feels is a chisel chopping away at it, cutting it and mutilating it. For example, let's take a piece of stone destined to be carved into a crucifix or a statue. We might ask it: "What do you think is happening to you?" And it might answer: "Don't ask me. All I know is that I must stay immobile in the hands of the sculptor. . . . I have no idea what he is doing, nor do I know what he will make of me. But what I do know is that his work is the best possible. It is perfect. I welcome each blow of his chisel as the best thing that could happen to me, although, if I'm to be truthful, I feel that every one of these blows is ruining me, destroying me, and disfiguring me."

Jean Pierre de Caussade

A PURE HEART

O Lord, let others ask for every kind of gift, with more and more prayers; I ask for one gift with but one prayer: "Grant me a pure heart!" How blessed are the pure of heart. By the power of their faith they see God within themselves; they see Him above and below, in all things, at all times. They become the instruments of this Divine Play, as God guides them everywhere and leads them to everything.

A pure heart and good will! The one foundation of every spiritual state! . . . The pure heart could well say to every soul: "Look at me carefully. It is I who generate that love which chooses the better part and clings to it; I produce that mild but effective fear which arouses such a detestation of evil that it can easily be avoided. I impart that excellent understanding which reveals the greatness of God and the merit of virtue. And it is also I who cause that passionate and holy yearning which keeps the soul resolute in virtue and in expectation of God."

Yes, O Pure Heart, you can invite everyone to gather round you and enrich themselves with your inexhaustible treasures. There is not one single kind of spiritual practice, not one path to holiness which does not find its source in you.

JEAN PIERRE DE CAUSSADE

FAITH

Faith transforms the earth into a paradise.
By it our hearts are raised with the joy
    of our nearness to heaven.
Every moment reveals God to us.
Faith is our light in this life.
By it we know the truth without seeing it,
    we are put in touch with what we cannot feel,
    recognize what we cannot see,
    and view the world stripped of all its outer shell.
    Faith unlocks God's treasury.
It is the key to all the vastness of His wisdom.
The emptiness of all created things is disclosed by faith,
    and it is by faith
    that God reveals Himself everywhere. . . .

With faith,
All that is dark becomes light,
    and what is bitter becomes sweet.
Faith transforms ugliness into beauty,
    and malice into kindness.
Faith is the mother of tenderness,
    trust, and joy. . . .

There is nothing faith cannot overcome;
It passes beyond all shadows
    and through the darkest clouds
    to reach the truth, which it embraces
    and can never be parted from.

Jean Pierre de Caussade

Come, then, my beloved souls,
    let us run and fly to that love which calls us.
Why are we waiting?
Let us set out at once,
    lose ourselves in the very heart of God
    and become intoxicated with His love.
Let us snatch from His heart the key
    to all the treasures of the world
    and start out right away on the road to heaven.
There is no need to fear
    that anything will be locked against us.
Our key will open every door.
There is no room we cannot enter.
We can make ourselves free of the garden,
    the cellar, and the vineyard too.
If we want to explore the countryside,
    no one will hinder us.
We can come and go,
    enter and leave anyplace we want to
    because we have
The key of David,
The key of knowledge,
And the key of the abyss,
    that holds all the hidden treasures
    of the divine wisdom.
It is this key that opens the doors of mystical death
    and its sacred darkness.
By it we can enter the deepest dungeons
    and emerge safe and sound.
It gives us entrance into that blessed spot

where the light of knowledge shines
and the Bridegroom takes His noonday rest.
There we quickly learn how to win His kiss
and ascend with surety the steps
of the nuptial couch.
And there we learn the secrets of love—
Divine secrets which cannot be revealed
and which no human tongue can ever describe.

Jean Pierre de Caussade

But what is the secret of finding this treasure?—There isn't one. This treasure is everywhere. It is offered to us all the time and wherever we are. All creatures, friends or foes, pour it out in abundance, and it flows through every fiber of our body and soul until it reaches the very core of our being. If we open our mouths they will be filled. God's activity runs through the universe. It wells up around and penetrates every created being. Where they are, there it is also. It goes ahead of them, it is with them, and it follows them. All they have to do is let its waves sweep them onward, fulfill the simple duties of their religion and state, cheerfully accept all the troubles they meet, and submit to God's will in all they have to do. . . . This is the true spirituality, which is valid for all times and for everyone. We cannot become truly good in a better, more marvelous, and yet easier way than by the simple use of the means offered us by God: the ready acceptance of all that comes to us at each moment of our lives.

POET-SAINTS OF INDIA

—

SHANKARACHARYA
TUKARAM
JNANESHWAR
BASAVANNA
AKKAMAHADEVI
MIRABAI
RAMDASA
SWAMI MUKTANANDA

ऋपट कांही एक
तुम्चें करितों की
दाऊं नेणें जडीबुर
नाहीं शिष्यशाखा
नव्हें मठपति । व
नाहीं देवार्चन ।
नाहीं वेताळ प्रसन
नव्हें पुराणिक । व
नेणें वाद घटापट
नाहीं जाळीत भण

When Joseph Campbell heard a theologian say, "God is dead," he replied, "Obviously you haven't been to India." India is a land brimming with God's presence: The air is thick with the ringing of temple bells, the recitation of scriptures, and the ecstatic chanting of God's holy name. But the treasure of India is not found in her temples or her holy waters, but in her Saints, who have found God living within their own hearts, and who tell all the world of this ecstatic union.

India's greatest philosopher, called "Teacher of the world," was **Shankaracharya** (686–718), a Saint who completely renewed the practice of Hinduism and established monastic orders in the four corners of India. His literary output was vast, including poems, hymns, scriptural commentaries, and the great philosophical treatise called *Vivekachudamani (The Crest-Jewel of Discrimination)*.

The "King of Saints" was *Jnaneshwar* (?1271–1293) who, while living only twenty-two years, made an indelible mark on the whole of Hindu spirituality. Until his time the scriptures of India were in the secret language of Sanskrit and unavailable to most people. Breaking from tradition, Jnaneshwar not only translated the *Bhagavad Gita* into Marathi, the common language, but also added a commentary, which now stands among the greatest spiritual works ever written.

Tukaram (?1598–?1650) was born into a family of poor peasants. Thanking God for his humble birth he wrote, "Well done, Lord! Had I been a learned man, pride and arrogance would have taken over and I would have scorned the service of the saints." Simple and direct, he was one of the great poets of the *Bhakti* movement, which stressed total devotion to God through chanting, worship, and the repetition of His Name.

Mirabai (1498–1546) was a Rajasthan princess famed for her love of Lord Krishna. Her "God-intoxicated" singing and dancing was considered a disgrace by her courtly relatives and they repeatedly tried to kill her. But, because of her great faith and devotion to God, Mirabai was always protected. *Akkamahadevi* (12th century), betrothed to the king of the land, was also oppressed by her royal surroundings and yearned only for union with her Lord. She eventually renounced her possessions and, in defiance of convention, wandered about with only the tresses of her hair as a covering. Her poems address three main forms of love—love withheld, love in separation, and love united—all to her chosen form of God, "The Lord White as Jasmine."

Basavanna (1106–1167) was an activist and social reformer who initiated a widespread movement that rejected the inequalities, customs, and caste system of Indian society. "Love of Shiva," he said, "cannot live with such restrictions." In all, one hundred and ninety thousand devotees are said to have been under Basavanna's direction. *Ramdasa* (1608–1681), the "Saint-errant," was the famed Guru of King Shivaji. In his brilliant work, the *Dasabodha,* he praises the company of the saints, tells of the greatness of God, and insists on the necessity of having a Guru.

Swami Muktananda (1908–1982) was a Saint from Ganeshpuri, India, whose writings capture the essence of all Indian spirituality. Although the words of great Masters are invaluable, Muktananda's greatest contribution will no doubt be his bringing the secret, and experience, of *Shaktipat* (the awakening of one's spiritual energy) to the West. He also established the present form of Siddha Yoga—a yoga based on chanting, meditation, service, and one's relationship to a perfect Master—which is practiced in ashrams and centers throughout the world.

SHANKARACHARYA

This Atman (the inner Self) shines with its own light. Its power is infinite. It is beyond sense-knowledge. It is the source of all experience. He who knows the Atman is free from every kind of bondage. He is full of glory. He is the greatest of the great.

Sometimes he appears to be a fool, sometimes a wise man. Sometimes he seems splendid as a king, sometimes feeble-minded. Sometimes he is calm and silent. Sometimes he draws men to him, as a python attracts his prey. Sometimes people honor him greatly, sometimes they insult him. Sometimes they ignore him. That is how the illumined soul lives, always absorbed in the highest bliss.

He has no riches, yet he is always contented. He is helpless, yet of mighty power. He enjoys nothing, yet he is continually rejoicing. He has no equal, yet he sees all men as his equals.

He acts, yet is not bound by action. He reaps the fruit of past actions, yet is unaffected by them. He has a body, yet does not identify himself with it. He appears to be an individual, yet he is present in all things, everywhere.

SHANKARACHARYA

A GARLAND OF QUESTIONS

What is the best thing a spiritual seeker can do?
Carry out his Guru's instructions.

What is the first and most important duty
for a man of right understanding?
To cut through the bonds of worldly desire.

To whom do the gods pay homage?
To one who is compassionate.

Who is deaf?
One who does not listen to good advice.

Who is dumb?
One who does not speak kind words
when they are needed.

What is most to be deplored?
Miserliness in the wealthy.

Wherein likes strength?
In patience.

Who profits from this life?
One who is humble.

Who is free from sin?
One who chants the name of the Lord.

SHANKARACHARYA

The treasure I have found cannot be described in words,
  the mind cannot conceive of it.
My mind fell like a hailstorm into that vast expanse
  of Consciousness.
Touching one drop of it I melted away and became one
  with the Absolute.
And now, though I return to human consciousness,
I see nothing, I hear nothing,
I know that nothing is different from me.

SHANKARACHARYA

THE SIX STANZAS OF SALVATION

I am neither the mind, the intellect,
   nor the whispering voice within;
Neither the eyes, the ears, the nose, nor the mouth.
I am not water, fire, earth, nor ether—
I am Consciousness and Bliss.
   I am Shiva! I am Shiva!

I am not the life-force nor the vital airs;
Not the seven components, nor the five sheaths;
I am not the tongue, hands, feet, nor organ
   of procreation—
I am Consciousness and Bliss.
   I am Shiva! I am Shiva!

Neither attachment nor aversion can touch me;
   neither greed, delusion, pride, nor jealousy are mine
   at all.
I am not duty, nor wealth, nor happiness—
I am Consciousness and Bliss.
   I am Shiva! I am Shiva!

I am not virtue nor vice, pain nor pleasure;
Neither temple nor holy word; neither sacred fire
   nor Veda—
I am Consciousness and Bliss.
   I am Shiva! I am Shiva!

I have neither death, nor doubt, nor class distinction;
No father, no mother, no birth at all.
I am not the brother, the friend, the guru, nor
    the disciple—
I am Consciousness and Bliss.
    I am Shiva! I am Shiva!

I am not detachment, salvation,
    nor anything reached by the senses;
I am beyond all thought and form;
I am everywhere, and nowhere at all—
I am Consciousness and Bliss.
    I am Shiva! I am Shiva!

TUKARAM

Now is the treasure unending
  laid open to all—
Come, take, and be rich.

Do not argue as to where
  that treasure may be,
Or what jewels lie therein—
Come, take, and be rich.

Soon, like a pot broken and worn,
  this body will grow old
But what the Master has to give
  remains forever new—
Come, take, and be rich.

No miserly doling of gifts with Him;
  like floods of water in a drought,
All that thy deepest soul needs
  is thine for the taking—
Come, take, and be rich.

TUKARAM

Of what use is all this restless, busy activity?
This heavy weight of worldly concerns?

God's purpose stands firm,
And you, His dear one,
Need but one thing—
Trust that He will fulfill your highest need.

All your burdens rest safe on Him,
And you, His dear one,
May play securely by His side.

This is the sum and substance of it all—
God alone is,
God alone loves thee,
God alone will bear all your cares.

TUKARAM

The servants of God are softer than wax and harder than a diamond. They are dead though living, and awake though sleeping. They will fulfill the desires of all, and give everyone what they want. . . . They will be more affectionate than parents, and work greater wrong than enemies. Nectar cannot be sweeter and poison more bitter than these Saints.

Even God dances before the singing Saint.
That incarnate of bliss,
    stands in the courtyard of the devotee.
The Saint does not care for liberation—
    liberation cares for the Saint.
As the Saint sleeps,
    God stands up to watch over him;
As the Saint sings God's Name,
    God nods His head with pleasure;
As the Saint stands up and utters the Name of God,
    God dances before him;
God indeed loves the chanting of His Name
    as nothing else,
And for the sake of this,
    He comes to the Saint's rescue at all times.

TUKARAM

The Saint becomes so unified with God,
    that it is impossible to distingush
    between God and Saint.
Embrace meets embrace.
Body is unified with body.
Words mix with words.
Eyes meet with eyes.

I have girdled up my loins,
    and have found out a way
    for you across the ocean of life.
Come here, come here,
    great and small,
    women and men.
Take no thought; have no anxiety.
I shall carry all of you to the other shore.
I come as the sole bearer of the stamp of God
    to carry you over in God's Name.

TUKARAM

He who utters the Name of God while walking,
    gets the merit of a sacrifice at every step.
Blessed is his body,
It is itself a place of pilgrimage.
He who says God's Name while doing his work,
    is always merged in perfect peace.
He who utters the Name of God while eating,
    gets the merit of a fast
    even though he may have taken his meals.
Even if one were to give in charity
    the whole earth encircled by the seas,
    that cannot equal the merit of repeating the Name.
By the power of the Name,
    one will know what cannot be known.
One will see what cannot be seen.
One will speak what cannot be spoken.
One will meet what cannot be met.
Tuka says,
    Incalculable is the gain which comes
    from repeating the Name of God.

TUKARAM

Deep has called unto deep
   and all things have vanished into unity.
The waves and the ocean have become one.
Nothing can come,
   and nothing can now pass away.
The Self is enveloping Himself all around.
The time of the Great End has come,
   sunset and sunrise have ceased . . .
All men have now become God,
   and merit and demerit have vanished. . . .

When one looks into a mirror,
   it seems as if one is looking at a different object,
   and yet one is looking at oneself.
I am the brook that has merged into the river.
My country is now the whole universe.

Liberation cannot be purchased in a market-place,
   nor can it be acquired
   by wandering in the woods or forests.
Liberation cannot be bought by large quantities of wealth,
   nor can it be found in the upper or nether worlds.
Liberation can be acquired,
   says Tuka,
   only at the cost of life.

JNANESHWAR

THE NECTAR OF SELF-AWARENESS

I honor the God and the Goddess,
The eternal parents of the universe.

The Lover, out of boundless love,
    takes the form of the Beloved.
What beauty!
Both are made of the same nectar
    and share the same food.

Out of Supreme Love
    they swallow each other up,
But separate again
    for the joy of being two.

They are not completely the same
    but neither are they different.
None can tell exactly what they are.

How intense is their longing
    to be with each other.
This is their greatest bliss.
Never, even in jest,
Do they allow their unity
    to be disturbed.

They are so averse to separation
That even though they have become
    this entire world,

Never for a moment do they let a difference
    come between them.

Even though they see
    all that is animate and inanimate,
    as arising from within themselves,
Never do they recognize a third.

They sit together
    in the same place,
Both wearing a garment of light.
From the beginning of time
    they have been together,
Reveling in their own Supreme Love.

The difference they created
    to enjoy this world
Had one glimpse of their intimacy
And could not help
    but merge back into the bliss
    found in their union.

Without the God
    there is no Goddess,
And without the Goddess
    there is no God.

How sweet is their love!
The entire universe
    is too small to contain them,
Yet they live happily
    in the tiniest particle.

The life of one
    is the life of the other,
And not even a blade of grass can grow
    without the both of them.

Only these two live
    in this house called the universe.
When either one is asleep
The other stays awake
    and plays the part of both.

Should either of them wake up
The whole universe would vanish
    without a trace.

They become two
    for the sake of a divine play,
But in every moment
    they seek to become one again.

Both of them see together,
Both of them are seen together.
They are happy
    only when together.

Shiva has become all forms:
    both dark and light,
    both male and female.
By the union of these two halves
    does the whole universe come to be.

Two lutes make one note.
Two roses make one fragrance.
Two lamps make one light.

Two lips—one word.
Two eyes—one sight.
Shiva and Shakti—one universe.

Though appearing separate
They are forever joined,
    always eating from the same plate.

She is a chaste and devoted partner;
    She cannot live without Her Lord.
And without Her,
    the one who can do everything,
    cannot even appear.

How can we distinguish these two from each other?
He appears because of Her,
And She exists because of Him.

We cannot tell sugar
    from its sweetness,
Nor camphor
    from its fragrance.

To capture light
    we take hold of fire.
To capture the Supreme Shiva
    we must take hold of Shakti.

Light illumines the Sun,
But the Sun itself
    creates that light.
The glorious Sun and its light
    are one and the same.

An object has a reflection:
When looking we see two,
    yet there is only one.
Likewise, this world is a reflection
    of the Supreme Lord,
You may see two,
Yet only one exists.

Out of pure emptiness
She gave rise to the entire world.
Everything depends on Her.
Yet She exists
    only because of Her Lord.

Her form is the whole world,
    it is the glory of God manifest.
God Himself created Her form,
God Himself became that form.

Seeing Herself beautifully adorned,
    She could not bear that Her Lord
    might have less than Herself.
And so She adorned Him
    with every name and form in the universe.

Merged in unity
    there was nothing to do.
So Shakti, the bringer of good fortune,
Created this world for the sake of divine play.

She reveals Her Lord's splendor,
    by melting Herself and becoming everything;
And He glorifies Her,
    by hiding Himself completely.

Out of His great love to see Her
    He becomes the Seer of the universe.
If He could not watch Her,
    He would have no reason to exist.

To meet Her call
    He takes on the form of the whole universe;
Without Her there
    He remains naked.

He is so mysterious and subtle,
That while apparent
    He cannot be seen.
It is by Her grace alone
    that He comes into being.

She awakens Her Lord,
    and serves Him a feast the size of the universe.
With great delight
    He swallows up every dish
    and also the one who serves Him.

While He is sleeping,
She gives birth to all that exists
    and all that does not exist.
When She is sleeping,
    He has no form whatsoever.

Look!
He is hidden,
    and cannot be found without Her.
For they are mirrors,
    each revealing the other.

Embracing Her,
Shiva enjoys His own bliss.
Though all the joy of the world belongs to Him,
There is no joy without Her.

She is His very form,
But Her radiance comes from Him.
Blending into one,
    they enjoy the nectar of their own union.

Shiva and Shakti are one,
Like air and the wind,
Like gold and its luster.

Shiva and Shakti cannot be separated.
They are like musk and its fragrance,
    like fire and its heat.

In the light of the Sun
    there is no difference between day and night.
In the Light of the Supreme Truth
    there is no difference between Shiva and Shakti.

Shiva and Shakti envy the Primordial Sound *Om*
    because they are regarded as two
    while the sound Om is always regarded as one.

Jnanadeva says,
"I honor the union of Shiva and Shakti,
    who devour this world of name and form
    like a sweet dish.
All that remains is the One."

Embracing each other
    they merge into One,
As darkness merges with the light
At the breaking of dawn.

When we discover their Unity
All words and all thoughts
    dissolve into silence,
Just as when the Universal Deluge comes,
    the waters of the ocean, and of the Ganges,
    will merge into one . . .

The air and the wind
    will merge into the endless sky;
The sun and its light
    will merge into the Universal Fire.

With a true vision of them,
    the seer and the seen
    merge into one.
Again I honor
    the two who are one.

They are like an ocean of knowledge.
And only those who throw themselves in can drink.

I appear separate from them
    just so I can honor them.
But that separation is not real,
    it is only in name.

My praise is like that of a gold ornament
    honoring the gold
    from which it is made.

When the tongue is used to pronounce the word *tongue*
Is there any difference between the word
    and the object meant by it?

One is called "Ocean,"
    the other is called "Ganges,"
    and though these are different names,
Their waters are still the same.

The sun can be seen,
    but so can the objects it illumines.
Does this mean there are two suns?

If moonlight shines on the surface of the moon,
Or if the light of a lamp reveals the lamp,
    can we claim that there is another?

The syllable *Om* is made up of the sounds *A, U,* and *M*:
    does that mean it is divided?
The letter *N* is made up of three lines,
    does that mean it is more than one?

When the luster of a pearl
    shines upon its surface
The pearl's beauty is only enhanced.

If one's bounty is not lessened,
    and only profit is obtained,
Why should the ocean not enjoy its waves,
    or a flower its own fragrance?

So I enjoy the worship of Shiva and Shakti,
    though I am never separate from them.

A reflected image disappears
　　when the mirror is removed,
Ripples merge back into the water
　　when the wind becomes still.

When sleep comes to an end
　　a man returns to his own senses.
Now my individuality has come to an end,
　　and I have returned to Shiva and Shakti.

Salt gives up its salty taste
　　to become one with the ocean;
I gave up my individual self
　　and became Shiva and Shakti.

When the covering is removed,
　　the air inside a plantain tree
　　merges with the air outside.
And this is how I honor Shiva and Shakti—
　　by removing all separation and
　　becoming one with them.

JNANESHWAR

Krishna

If it is said that I am concealed by the existence of the world, then who is it that blossoms in the form of the world? Can a red jewel be concealed by its own luster? Does a chip of gold lose its goldness if turned into an ornament? Does a lotus lose itself when it blossoms into so many petals? When a seed of grain is sown and grows into an ear of corn, is it destroyed or does it appear in its enhanced glory? So there is no need to draw the curtain of the world away in order to have my vision, because I am the whole panorama.

JNANESHWAR

Krishna

Therefore, giving up the conception of difference, a person should know Me alongside himself. He should not regard himself as different from Me, as a speck of gold is not different from the whole block of gold. He should understand well how a ray of light, though proceeding from an origin, is continuous with it. Like molecules on the surface of the earth, or flakes of snow on the Himalaya, all individual souls dwell in Me. A ripple, small or great, is not different from water. So he should know himself as not different from Me. Such insight is called Devotion. This is the supreme knowledge, the essence of all Yoga.

Basavanna

The rich
will make temples for Shiva.
What shall I,
a poor man,
do?

My legs are pillars,
the body the shrine,
the head a cupola
of gold.

Listen, O Lord of the meeting rivers,
things standing shall fall,
but the moving ever shall stay.

BASAVANNA

Make of my body the beam of a lute
of my head the sounding gourd
of my nerves the strings
of my fingers the plucking rods.

Clutch me close
and play your thirty-two songs
O lord of the meeting rivers!

AKKAMAHADEVI

You are the forest

you are all the great trees
    in the forest

you are bird and beast
    playing in and out
    of all the trees

        O lord white as jasmine
        filling and filled by all

        why don't you
        show me your face?

AKKAMAHADEVI

The heart in misery
has turned
upside down.

The blowing gentle breeze
is on fire.
O friend moonlight burns
like the sun.

Like a tax-collector in a town
I go restlessly here and there.

Dear girl go tell Him
bring Him to His senses.
Bring Him back.

My lord white as jasmine
is angry
that we are two.

Akkamahadevi

It was like a flood of water
pouring into the dry bed
of a lake,
like a torrent of rain
soaking every plant
parched and lifeless.

It was like the pleasures of the world
and the path to liberation,
both
rushing toward me.

Seeing the face of the master,
my Lord white as jasmine,
I saw,
I knew,
I became
everything!

MIRABAI

O Bountiful Lord,
　Listen!
Can you not hear my prayer?
Can you not hear your Name
　ever upon my lips?

My whole family has turned against me,
　And I am only a burden to them.
In all the worlds,
　I have no one but you
　to call my own.

O Lord,
　steer my tiny boat—
　the waters are dark and stormy.
I cannot find rest until you come to me.
The nights are endless—
　I lie in my bed,
　without chance of sleep.
Open your door,
　I beg you.
The shaft of separation
　has split open my breast
　and the pain will not leave
　for even a moment.

Did you not restore life to Ahalya,
    frozen in stone by a sage's curse?
Beneath your magic touch,
    she was raised up,
        blossoming with such beauty.
Why then don't you come and raise me up?
Am I not lighter than a statue of stone?

MIRABAI

You alone can break the cord
   that binds us now—
No one but you.
O Krishna,
You are the tree,
   I, the bird that nests in your branches.
You are the ocean,
   I, the fish that swims in your deeps.
You are the hill,
   I, the peacock who dances on your top.
You are the full moon,
   I, the *chakor* bird
   that never turns its gaze from your light.
You are the gold,
   I, the powder rubbed on to make you shine.
O my Master,
   Thou art Lord of the three worlds,
I am Mirabai,
   the one who sings your song,
   hoping you will hear me.

Mirabai

O Beloved,
   Let us go to that place,
   Let us go there together.

Tell me, what shall I wear?
   A golden sari,
   with a yellow flower behind my ear?
Or shall it be a simple dress,
   with a string of pearls
   along the part of my hair?

Let me be your handmaid;
I will plant myself in your garden,
   and there I will look upon your face
   and sing your praises forever.
Let me be your servant,
   and let my only wages
   be the sweetness of your Name.

I have dreamt of you
   since the world began,
With a crown of peacock feathers on your head,
With robes of amber and yellow.
I see a garland of roses around your neck
   as you take the cows out to graze.

O Krishna,
   Charmer of hearts,
   Lifter of mountains,
I hear your flute calling me—

Shall I come by the secret path
    through the tall grass?
O Lord of Heavenly Blue,
My heart cannot rest until we are together,
    until we walk along the banks of the Jamuna
    deep into the night.

RAMDASA

BRAHMAN

Brahman is always before all things.
It fills the whole universe.
To its immaculateness, there is no comparison.
In all heavens, in the celestial worlds,
    from the far reaches of the earth,
        it fills every nook and cranny.
It fills all this space at once. It touches all,
    and abides in all.
It cannot be soiled by clay.
It cannot be carried away by flood.
Simultaneously, it is before us and behind us.
Simultaneously, it is to our right and to our left.
Simultaneously, it is above and below.

As soon as we begin to be aware of it,
    we forget it.
But as soon as we forget it,
    it comes within the ken
    of our consciousness. . . .

When we try to realize it,
    It cannot be realized.
When we try to leave it,
    It cannot be left.
We are connected with Brahman forever
    and this connection is unbreakable.

Ramdasa

BRAHMAN

Brahman is more spotless than the sky.
It is as formless as it is vast.
It extends above all heavens.
It exists beyond all worlds.
There is not the smallest part of the universe
    which it does not occupy.
It is quite near to us,
    and yet it is hidden.
We live in it,
    and yet we do not know it.

Wherever you cast your glance,
    it is before you.
You in fact see within it.
It is both inside and outside.
Where we feel it is not,
    it immediately manifests itself.
Whatever object we take in hand—
    it is nearer to us than that.

Ramdasa says,
Only he can know this secret,
    who has had the spiritual experience himself.

RAMDASA

REAL KNOWLEDGE

Knowledge of all the sciences is not real knowledge. To distinguish a good horse from a bad one, to know the various classes of animals, to know every kind of bird, is not real knowledge. To know the various metals, to know the various coins, to know the various jewels, is not real knowledge. To know various words, to know various languages, is not real knowledge. To speak straight away, to have ready wit, to compose poetry extempore, is not real knowledge. To know the art of singing, to know the art of dancing, is not real knowledge. To know the various kinds of pictures, to know the various kinds of instruments, to know the various kinds of arts, is not real knowledge. All this is only a product of the mind. That knowledge by which a man attains liberation, that is real knowledge—it is of a different kind altogether.

RAMDASA

THE IDEAL MAN

The Ideal Man loves to put forth effort,
    enters boldly on any enterprise,
    and does not shun work.
He can live in the midst of difficulties,
    bear the brunt of action,
    and yet keeps himself away from contact with it.

He is everywhere,
      and yet nowhere.

Like Atman, he hides himself. Nothing
    can take place without his mediation;
                yet he is not himself seen.

Those who follow the instructions of a wise man
    themselves become wise.
That is the justification of the existence of a wise man.
He always supports the right cause,
    and never gives himself to falsehood.
In the midst of difficulties, he knows the way out.

A man of courage is a great support to all.
This indeed is what he has become
    through the Grace of God.

Ramdasa

SAINTS

The Saints indeed are truly the rich;
　　for they possess in their hands
　　the keys of the spiritual treasure.
The spiritually poor have been made by them
　　spiritual Kings of men. . . .
Emperors and kings have lived erewhile,
　　but none of them
　　has been able to make a grant of God;
Only the Saints can confer this boon.
There is no limit to the greatness of the Saints,
　　for it is on account of them
　　that God reveals Himself.
The Saints have within them
　　the power to give what no one else can give—
The secret knowledge of the Godhead.
What is impossible to be attained by
　　ordinary means
Becomes possible only by contact with the Saints.

RAMDASA

THE GURU

Without a great Guru
 we cannot attain to our intimate treasure.
Without the grace of the Guru
 one cannot realize the Self.
Contemplation and concentration,
devotion and worship,
 are all useless
 without the grace of the Guru.
Without the grace of the Guru,
 one moves like a blind man, floundering,
 falling into ditches
 as he wends his way.

All great men that have lived in bygone times,
All the Saints and Sages of old
 have attained realization
 only by the power of the Guru.

In short,
Liberation can be attained
 only by the help of a Guru
 and in no other way.

SWAMI MUKTANANDA

PERFECT BEINGS

The state of a Siddha is beyond both knowing and not knowing. In that state, bliss is embraced by bliss. Joy is experienced through joy. Success is gained through success. Light dwells within light. . . . In that state, astonishment drowns in astonishment. All dos and don'ts are silenced. Rest attains total rest. Experience delights in experience. The state of a Siddha is the attainment of total perfection. Siddhas are like this. O friend, read this very carefully.

If a person with a taintless heart and a vigilant and pure mind keeps the company of a Siddha for just a moment, half a moment, or even half of that, he can instantly go across the ocean of mundane existence. . . . Only by becoming a fish can one know how a fish lives. To understand a great being, one first has to become one with him. That is true knowledge.

Swami Muktananda

THE GURU

When a disciple surrenders himself to the Guru, the Guru takes full responsibility for his progress. The Guru guarantees that he will lead the disciple to the goal.

If you understand what I am going to tell you, you won't have to work very hard, you won't even have to meditate very much. The Guru is not a physical form. The Guru is not an impressive figure peering at you from a picture. The Guru is not a person with long hair or a beard. The Guru is the divine power of Grace. The Guru is Shakti Herself. Even if you receive Shakti from the Guru, it is not his personal possession. The Shakti comes from the divine source, from the Supreme Lord, and this you must never forget.

If you do not have this knowledge, no matter how much you meditate, it will not lead you anywhere. If you are ignorant of the nature of Shakti, no matter how much wealth you have, you are poor. All that you need, wherever you are, is this constant awareness of the true nature of the Shakti, firm faith in it, and true devotion to it. If you have such firm faith, Shakti will guide you wherever you may be; Shakti will take the form of the Guru, or Shakti will give you messages from within. You will have absolutely no difficulty.

The world is a creation of Shakti, and a spiritual seeker, a meditator, should not look down upon the world or regard it as something other than Shakti. Shakti does not only manifest Herself as Divine Energy within the body; it is Shakti who projects the cosmos in the pure void. It is Shakti who makes this world while staying different from this world. It is Shakti who becomes good as well as bad. It is Shakti who manifests Herself in our worldly pursuits and also in our spiritual pursuits. So we should not regard our mundane life as being different from Shakti. That is an aspect of the same Shakti we are trying to attain through meditation. The Shakti creates the universe and dwells in a human being in the form of Divine Energy. A yogi worships Her and awakens Her. So nothing is really different or apart from the Shakti. Wherever you are you will receive guidance from the Shakti, because Shakti Herself manifests as your worldly life.

Swami Muktananda

THE WORLD

This world is the beautiful Garden of Shiva, of the Lord, made so that you can walk in it with great joy. . . . Why do you find unhappiness in it? If there were no joy in this world, then God would not have created it with so much love and effort. So there is some mistake in your understanding and in your behavior—that is why when you look at the world you see unhappiness. So improve your vision, and then you will understand that the world is God.

God is everywhere, there's no doubt about that, but you have to have the right eye to see Him. Look at the air. It blows everywhere, but you can't see it. You can only feel it when it touches you. . . . God can be seen. Sit quietly for a while and meditate on the Self. You'll be able to see Him. In what form would you like to see God? He has taken the form of bread in this piece of bread—don't try to see Him as a stone in bread. In fruit you should see God as fruit, in a tree you should see God as a tree, and in yourself you should see Him as yourself. Who says that God cannot be seen? Don't try to see Him as different from the way He has manifested Himself—see Him as He is! Try to see Him as he is.

SWAMI MUKTANANDA

LOVE

Love is our only reason for living and the only purpose of life. We live for the sake of love, and we live seeking love. For the sake of love an actor performs, and for the sake of love a writer writes. For the sake of love a sensualist enjoys the pleasures of the body, and for the sake of love a meditator turns within and isolates himself from the world. Everything we do in life we do with the hope of experiencing love. We say, "If I do not find it today, perhaps I will find it tomorrow. If I do not find it in this person, perhaps I will find it in that one." Love is essential for all of us.

It is not surprising that we keep looking for love, because we are all born of love. We come out of love. All of us are nothing but vibrations of love. We are sustained by love, and in the end we merge back into love. . . . This world is nothing but a school of love; our relationships with our husband or wife, with our children and parents, with our friends and relatives are the university in which we are meant to learn what love and devotion truly are.

Yet the love we experience through other people is just a shadow of the love of the inner Self. There is a sublime place inside us where love dwells. . . . The love that pulses in the cave of the heart does not depend on anything outside. It does not expect anything. It is completely independent.

The love of the Self is selfless and unconditional. It is not relative. It is completely free. It is self-generated and it never dies. This kind of love knows no distinction between high and low, between man and woman. Just as the earth remains the same no matter who comes and goes on it, so true love remains unchanging and independent. Love penetrates your entire being. Love is Consciousness. Love is bliss. It does not exist for the sake of something else. It is supremely free. The path of inner love leads a lover to God. As a person walks on this inner path of love he not only attains love, but merges in the ocean of love.

If you want to experience love, you have to start by loving yourself. First you have to love your body, then those who are related to your body, and then the master of the body, the inner Self. . . . The truth is that God has no physical body; the only body He has is the body of love. If the love you experience in your daily life—the little love you feel for your friends, your relatives, your pets, and even your possessions—could be turned toward the inner Self, that would be enough to bring you liberation.

SWAMI MUKTANANDA

THE UNIVERSAL ENERGY

Chiti is supremely free. She is self-revealing. She is the only cause of creation, sustenance, and dissolution of the universe. She exists, holding the power within Her that creates, sustains, and destroys. The prime cause of everything, She is also the means to the highest bliss. All forms, all places, and all instants of time are manifested from Her. She is all-pervading, always completely full and of everlasting light. Manifesting as the universe, still She remains established in Her indivisibility and unity. Within the Blue Light, She pulsates as ambrosial bliss. There is nothing apart from Her. There is no one like Her. She is only One, the supreme witness, the One who is called cosmic consciousness or Supreme Shiva. She is ever solitary. In the beginning, in the middle, and in the end, only Chiti is. She does not depend on any other agency; She is Her own basis and support. As She alone exists, She is in perfect freedom.

Swami Muktananda

PLAY OF CONSCIOUSNESS

As I gazed at the tiny Blue Pearl, I saw it expand, spreading its radiance in all directions so that the whole sky and earth were illuminated by it. It was now longer a Pearl but had become shining, blazing, infinite Light; the Light which the writers of the scriptures and those who have realized the Truth have called the divine Light of Chiti. The Light pervaded everywhere in the form of the universe. I saw the earth being born and expanding from the Light of Consciousness, just as one can see smoke rising from a fire. I could actually see the world within this conscious Light, and the Light within the world, like threads in a piece of cloth, and cloth in the threads. Just as a seed becomes a tree, with branches, leaves, flowers, and fruit, so within Her own being Chiti becomes animals, birds, germs, insects, gods, demons, men, and women. I could see this radiance of Consciousness, resplendent and utterly beautiful, silently pulsating as supreme ecstasy within me, outside me, above me, below me.

THE KINGDOM WITHIN

All philosophies and scriptures say the same thing: "In this human body it is God who dwells."

Do not consider your body a mere lump of flesh made of seven components. It is a noble instrument. In it are situated all holy places, gods, mantras, and the source of all extraordinary powers in this world. . . . God dwells in the body. He is present as fully in you as in the highest heavens. Why are you exhausting yourself looking for Him in different places instead of in your own heart? You should live your normal life, but accord Him the chief place among your daily activities. Whatever may be your religion or philosophy, do not make yourself a foolish, weak, and trivial creature. Do not head towards decline and disaster by regarding this body as godless. Do not commit spiritual suicide by belittling yourself through defective understanding.

There are many different phenomena inside the human body. If a man were to see the inner splendor in meditation even once, he would derive immense benefit from it. How wonderful the treasures within this body! Pools of nectarean juices! Numberless sheaves of sensory nerves! Reverberating musical concerts! Varied intoxicating perfumes! Countless rays of different suns! Sacred dwellings of gods! In spite of such wealth, man goes looking for sweet happiness in the external world and ends up weary and joyless.

The universe within is superior to that without. How wonderful the seat of clairaudience in the ear! How significant the center of deep sleep in the throat, that easily dissolves the fatigue of the waking hours. . . . In your heart there is a lotus whose different petals stand for different qualities such as anger, infatuation, greed, love, modesty, knowledge, joy, and so on. Sages have spent their whole lives trying to behold the scintillating divine light that lies within the heart. How glorious the Goddess Kundalini who transforms a man as She expands! O soul of man! What joy could beckon you in the external world while such an infinite treasure of marvels lies within?

When the latent treasure of inner Shakti is released in meditation, you will soon ascend to the higher meditative stages. You will see splendid sights and glorious forms. You will perceive internal divine lights. It is only by virtue of these lights that your body becomes beautiful and you feel love for one another. As the magnificent radiance sparkles in meditation, your craving for beautiful and loving forms will be satisfied. You will see the whole world as radiant.

Along with visions, you will hear inner sounds. Sweet, divine music will ring in your ears. As you listen to it, you will have such sleep as is enjoyed only by heavenly beings. These melodious strains will compel you to dance in ecstasy and eradicate your indifference, distress, and ramblings of mind. Not only this, the inner music will release celestial ambrosia and you will relish its sweetness. This nectar, trickling from the palate, is the sweetest of all tastes. Each drop of it is worth more than millions. This elixir will expel all your diseases and fill you with gladness. Your anguish will vanish. You will exude ambrosial sweetness. You will rejoice in your spouse and children. As you taste this nectar and become absorbed in it, you will be transported with inner delight.

O my dear ones! You will also inhale divine scents. As your inner aroma is released, not only your home but your whole world will become tranquil; your body will shed its heaviness and sloth, and become lithe and vibrant.

When your inner Kundalini Shakti is stirred, She will release Her impulses of love throughout your body and its seventy-two thousand nerves. She will thrill your every blood cell with Her ecstatic joy. Only then will your craving for touch be truly gratified. You will recover the lost luster of your eyes. Your withered face will again glow with love and your lips will become rosy. Your world will quiver with beauty, joy, and love! You will become aware of the omnipresence of the Lord; you will realize that this entire world is His and He is maintaining it.

My dearest ones! Do not give up your worldly life, your near and dear ones. Do not waste yourselves away, rushing around in search of God in the four directions, nor lose your own souls while seeking inner peace and comfort. Live in your own homes with your spouses and children, making full use of your artistic talents, running your businesses or factories. In whatever position your destiny has placed you, whether you are millionaires or laborers, kings or beggars, God belongs to you all. If you call Him with love, thinking about Him with devotion, He will reveal Himself to you. He will grant a vision of the divine light of His love. Then you will know that you are an embodiment of bliss. You will realize, "I am Shiva! Yes I am! Yes I am!"

JNANESHWAR

May the Self of the universe be pleased
With this sacrifice of words
And bestow His grace upon me.

May sinners no longer commit evil deeds,
May their desire to do good increase,
And may all beings live in harmony with one another.

May the darkness of sin disappear,
May the world see the rising of the sun of righteousness,
And may the desires of all creatures be satisfied.

May everyone keep the company of
    The saints devoted to God,
Who will shower their blessings on them.

Saints are the walking gardens
Filled with wish-fulfilling trees,
And they are the living villages
Of wish-fulfilling gems.
Their words are like oceans of nectar.
They are moons without blemish
And suns without heat.
May these saints be the friends of all people.

May all beings in the world be filled with joy,
And may they worship God forever . . .

Then the great Master said,
This blessing will be granted.
This brought great joy to Jnaneshwar.

GLOSSARY

Ahalya (India, ?5th century B.C.)
A woman who, according to legend, was frozen in stone by a sage's curse for infidelity and brought back to life by the touch of Lord Krishna.

Arjuna (India, ?5th century B.C.)
Famed archer and warrior prince to whom Lord Krishna imparted the teachings of the *Bhagavad Gita*.

Ashram (Sanskrit)
From the Sanskrit, *a*, "without," and *shram*, "fatigue"; a place where discipline and spiritual practices are followed; the abode of a Guru or Master. A typical ashram schedule includes early morning meditation (4:30 A.M.), chanting of sacred texts, selfless service *(seva)*, and study of the truth *(satsang)*.

Atman (Sanskrit)
The inner Self; Divine Consciousness residing in the individual; the Soul.

In half a verse I will tell you what is contained in a million scriptures: Brahman (the Absolute Reality) alone is real, the world is unreal; the Atman and Brahman are one. (Shankaracharya)

Bhakti (Sanskrit)

The fastest and most assured path to enlightenment, *bhakti* is complete absorption, total devotion, and supreme love of God or one's Guru. The definitive text on *bhakti* is *The Bhakti Sutras of Narada,* which states:

This Love is devoid of qualities, seeks no return, grows from more to more every moment, knows no break, is subtler than the subtlest and is of the nature of experience. Attaining this Love, the loving devotee sees nothing but Love, hears only about Love, speaks only of Love, and thinks of Love alone.

Brahman (Sanskrit)

The all-pervasive Absolute Reality; God, *Shiva* (Sanskrit), *Allah* (Arabic).

Buddha (Sanskrit)

Literally the "Awakened One," it is a Buddhist term for an enlightened being. It also refers to the historic founder of Buddhism who lived in the sixth century B.C. and was called *Siddhartha Gautama,* the name given to him at birth; *Shakyamuni Buddha,* the name he received during his travels, meaning, "Silent Sage of the Shakyas"; and *Tathagata,* the name he used when referring to himself, meaning "the Perfect One."

Chiti (Sanskrit)

The ever-creative power of God; Consciousness in the form of the supreme energy that gives rise to the universe; *Shakti* (Sanskrit), *Sophia* (Greek).

Confucius (551 B.C.–479 B.C.)

The most influential Chinese philosopher and founder of

Confucianism, a humanistic approach to life which emphasizes kindness, love of one's neighbor, and proper moral conduct.

Dharma (Sanskrit)

From the Sanskrit root *dhr*, "to sustain," "to uphold," or "to nourish," *dharma* is that which sustains life, the inherent laws of the world, and the divine order of the universe. It is most often associated with one's duty—how one sustains his own livelihood—however, on an inner level, *dharma* refers to living in harmony with the natural flow of the universe. *Dharma* is action that pleases the Lord; action that leads a soul to union with God—and this most often *is* one's duty in life. In the *Bhagavad Gita,* Krishna says, "Devoted to one's duty, man obtains perfection."

Dharma is a universal concept and often translated as "virtue." The New Jerusalem Bible says: "*virtue* is to be understood as perfect accord of mind and act with the divine will as manifested in the precepts of the law and injunctions of conscience." The Chinese called this perfect accord *Te*—the manifestation of Tao in a person; the Greeks, *eudaimonia*—"a good god within"; the Hebrews, *sedeq*—"righteousness," the keeping of God's Laws.

Dhyana Yoga (Sanskrit)

The yoga of meditation, based on focusing the mind on a given object, one's Guru, one's breath, or on the space between the breaths. Zen Buddhism has its roots in this form of yoga: the word *dhyana* in Sanskrit becomes *Ch'an* in Chinese and later *Zen* in Japanese.

Guru (Sanskrit)

From the Sanskrit *gu*, "darkness," and *ru*, "light." A Guru is a particular kind of enlightened being who has the power to dispel the *darkness* of ignorance with the *light* of the truth. This Supreme power of Grace that the Guru wields is the very essence of all attainments and realizations.

> He alone is the real Guru who leads a disciple to liberation. (Ramdasa)

> Who is a guru?
> One who is totally established in the truth of Brahman, and constantly acting for the benefit of his disciples. (Shankaracharya)

Karma (Sanskrit)

From the Sanskrit root *kr*, "action," karma is any action of the body, mind, or speech, and the result of that action.

To every action there is an equal and opposite reaction; and the individual soul must reap the fruits of its actions. Every self-motivated action—be it good or bad—binds one to this world. It is not through performance of good deeds but only through selfless service, and dedicating all one's actions to God, that one is freed from the bonds of karma. However, the storehouse of karma, accumulated in this lifetime and in previous lifetimes, is so vast that one must not only stop its creation but also "burn it up." Spiritual practices such as mantra repetition, chanting of God's Name, service to one's Master, and meditation on the Self, all have the power to burn up the bonds of karma.

Karma can be summed up thus: "As you sow, so shall you reap."

Karma Yoga (Sanskrit)

The yoga of selfless service *(seva);* dedicating the fruits of one's actions to God. The *Bhagavad Gita* is the supreme text of karma yoga, which says that man has the right to work but not to the fruits of his actions. In his commentary on the *Gita,* Jnaneshwar tells more about this mysterious yoga:

When the sun rises and sets, it seems to move although it is actually motionless. In the same way, realize that freedom from action lies in action. Such a person seems like other people, but he is not affected by human nature, like the sun which cannot be drowned in water. He sees the world without seeing it, does everything without doing it, and enjoys all pleasures without being involved in them. . . .

The walking of his feet, the speaking of his mouth, and all his other actions are the Supreme moving through him. Furthermore, he sees the whole universe as not different from himself. So how can action affect him? . . . He is free in every way and, even though he acts, he is free from action. Though he possesses attributes, he is beyond all attributes. There is no doubt about this.

Krishna (India, ?5th century B.C.)
From the Sanskrit meaning "the dark one," or "the one who attracts irresistibly," Krishna was an incarnation of God who came to re-establish righteousness in the world. His life is described in the Indian scripture the *Srimad Bhagavatam,* and his teachings on yoga, given to Arjuna on the battlefield, are contained in the *Bhagavad Gita.*

Kundalini (Sanskrit)
From the Sanskrit meaning, "the coiled one," the kundalini is a particularized form of the creative energy of the universe *(Shakti)* that lies dormant at the base of the spine in every human being. Once this "serpent energy" is awakened by the grace of a Master it journeys up through the central channel of the subtle body—removing all physical, mental, and spiritual blocks—and finally enters the spiritual center in the crown of the head. Once

this happens the individual self merges with the universal Self and enlightenment is attained.

Mahakashyapa (India, 5th century B.C.)
Foremost disciple of the historical Buddha and considered the first patriarch of the Indian lineage of Zen *(Ch'an)* Buddhism.

Mansur Mastana (Persia, 858–922)
A Sufi saint from Baghdad, who was hanged as a heretic by the orthodox of Islam for his proclamation *Ana'l Haq,* "I am God."

Mantra (Sanskrit)
A sacred word or sound infused with the power of God; a Name of God; the Supreme Being in the form of sound.

Correct repetition of a mantra is not only the repetition of a sacred word, but the continual awareness that the Guru who imparted the mantra, the one repeating the mantra, the mantra itself, and the Supreme Lord are one and the same. Only with this awareness will the mantra have the power to purify, protect, redeem, and ultimately give realization to the one who repeats it. A mantra taken from a book or from one who has not realized its full potential is useless; it is much like plugging an appliance into a wall outlet that is not supplied by electricity.

Maya (Sanskrit)
The Sanskrit word for God's power of illusion that brings about the whole world. This power causes the individual soul to believe that the unreal is real and that the transient is everlasting.

Maya is one of God's five powers, which are Creation, Sustenance, Dissolution, Concealment (Maya), and Revealing what has been concealed.

Name
God in the form of sound; the creative energy of God that

creates this entire universe. Also called the Word; *Logos* (Greek) and *Shakti* (Sanskrit).

> In the beginning was the Word, and the Word was with God, and the Word was God. (St. John)

Om (Sanskrit)
The primordial sound vibration of the universe and the essence of all mantras.

Shakti (Sanskrit)
The all-pervasive, creative energy of the Absolute Being; the power of Shiva. Also called *Chiti* (Sanskrit), *Sophia* (Greek), and *Te* (Chinese). The form of this supreme energy, that illumines the human body and—when awakened by a Master—removes every physical and spiritual block on the path to enlightenment, is called *kundalini*.

Shaktipat (Sanskrit)
Literally, "the descent of shakti." Specifically it refers to the transmission of spiritual energy from Master to disciple, and the awakening of the *kundalini* energy, which lies dormant at the base of the spine. This awakening is the single most important step for one seeking liberation. Shaktipat can be given in four ways: by the Guru's touch, word, look, or will.

Shiva (Sanskrit)
The all-pervasive, Supreme Reality; the Absolute; God; *Brahman* (Sanskrit); *Allah* (Arabic); *Tao* (Chinese). *Shiva* is said to be the Eternal Witness of the Universe and is often paired with *Shakti,* who creates this eternal dance for *Shiva*'s delight.

Shiva is also the name for one of the gods in the Hindu trinity, representing God's power of destruction.

Siddha (Sanskrit)
From the Sanskrit, meaning "perfect"; a perfect being; one who has attained Self-realization.

Siddha Yoga (Sanskrit)

The yoga (path to union with God) based on one's relationship with a perfect Master, both outwardly and inwardly. This is the yoga of grace, which encompasses all the other forms of yoga and unfolds spontaneously in the disciple once his dormant spiritual energy has been awakened.

Although existing in unbroken lineage for thousands of years, it was shaped into a set of practices and teachings and brought to the West by Swami Muktananda. When he died in 1982, the power of the lineage was passed on to his successor, Gurumayi Chidvilasananda.

Six Realms of Experience (Buddhism)

The realms of experience that beings go through on the endless cycle of birth and death; these are the realms of hell, unhappy ghosts, beasts, demons, humans, and celestial beings.

Sophia (Greek)

The Supreme Creative Power of God; the source of all wisdom; *Chiti* (Sanskrit), *Shakti* (Sanskrit), and *Te* (Chinese).

Sufi (Persian)

One who belongs to the mystical sect of Islam based on love and devotion.

Tao (Chinese)

A symbolic word from the Chinese that literally means "path," or "way," *Tao* is used to designate the one, impersonal, formless Absolute, from which the entire universe has evolved and to which it will return.

Te (Chinese)

The universal power *Tao* embodied in a form or acting through a person; the qualities or virtues a thing receives from *Tao* making it what it is. A literal translation, derived from the Chinese pictograph, might read: "perfect action of mind and heart" or "a heart and mind that do not deviate from the truth." Most often, however, *Te* is translated as "virtue," in the classic sense of the Latin word *virtus,* meaning the "inherent quality or power latent in a thing." However *Te* is not a moral concept, but a clear reflection of the virtues of the universe, such as goodness, love, compassion, generosity, and humility.

> The result of a pure eye is sight; the result of a pure ear is hearing; the result of a pure mouth is taste; the result of a pure mind is wisdom; the result of pure wisdom is Te. (Chuang Tzu)

Vedas (Sanskrit)
From the Sanskrit meaning "knowledge," or "sacred teachings," the Vedas are the sacred Scriptures that form the foundation of the Hindu religion. The four Vedas are the *Rigveda,* the Veda of hymns; the *Yajurveda,* the Veda of sacrificial texts; the *Samaveda,* the Veda of songs; and the *Atharvaveda,* the Veda of Artharva, overseer of the sacred fire ceremony.

Vishnu (Sanskrit)
The Supreme Lord who sustains the righteousness and truth of the universe.

Yoga (Sanskrit)
From the Sanskrit *yug,* meaning "union," yoga is the practice that leads the individual soul to union with God. This union can be accomplished in many different ways: *bhakti yoga* (union through devotion); *dhyana yoga* (union through meditation); *hatha yoga* (union through purification of the subtle body); *japa yoga* (union through the repetition of a sacred word); *karma yoga* (union through selfless service); *siddha yoga* (union through the grace of a Master).

Zen (Japanese)

A school of Buddhism that stresses the importance of enlightenment through the practice of *zazen,* sitting in a meditative, thought-free state. Essential to Zen practice is the special transmission from Master to disciple, looking into the nature of one's own mind, and direct experience of knowledge.

SOURCES

Three different terms are used when referring to works in this collection: *Translation*, when the work's primary source is a manuscript in the original language; *rendition*, when the work is produced by rewording or reformulating one or more existing translations; and *adaptation*, when the work is produced by editing or correcting one previous translation.

SCRIPTURES OF INDIA

Rig Veda

Rendered by Jonathan Star from Book X, 129.

Sources:

John M. Koller, *Oriental Philosophies* (New York: Scribner's Sons, 1985).

Swami Prabhavananda, *The Spiritual Heritage of India* (Hollywood, Calif.: Vedanta Press, 1979).

Arthur A. Macdonell, *A Vedic Reader* (London: Oxford University Press, 1917).

Upanishads

All selections rendered by Jonathan Star.
Selection on page 5 from the Shvetashvatara Upanishad.
Selection on pages 6–8 from the Chandogya Upanishad.
Selection on page 9 from the Mandukya Upanishad.

Sources:

Swami Prabhavananda and F. Manchester, trans., *The Upanishads, Breath of the Eternal* (Hollywood, Calif.: Vedanta Press, 1948).

D. S. Sharma, trans., *The Upanishads, an Anthology* (Bombay, India: Bharatiya Vidya Bhavan, 1961).

Robert E. Hume, trans., *The Thirteen Principle Upanishads* (London: Oxford University Press, 1921).

Sri Purohit Swami and W. B. Yeats, trans., *The Ten Principle Upanishads* (London: Faber and Faber, 1937).

Bhagavad Gita

Selection on pages 10–14 from Chapter 10, translated by Jonathan Star.
Selection on pages 15–19 from Chapter 11, translated by Jonathan Star.
Selection on pages 20–21 from Chapter 18, translated by Jonathan Star and Julle Lal.

Sources consulted:

Barbara Stoller Miller, trans., *The Bhagavad-Gita* (New York: Bantam Doubleday Dell, 1986).

Winthrop Sargeant, trans., *The Bhagavad Gita* (Albany, N.Y.: SUNY Press, 1984).

Swami Tapasyananda, trans., *Srimad Bhagavadgita* (Mylapore, Madras: Sri Ramakrishna Math, 1984).

Anilbaran Roy, ed., *The Gita* (Pondicherry, India: Sri Aurobindo Ashram, 1946).

Swami Prabhavananda and Christopher Ishwerood, trans., *The*

Song of God: *Bhagavad Gita* (Hollywood, Calif.: Vedanta Press, 1944).

S. Radhakrishnan, trans., *The Bhagavad Gita* (New York: Harper & Row, 1948).

Guru Gita

All selections translated by Julle Lal.

Vishnu Sahasranam

Rendered by Jonathan Star.

Sources:

Swami Muktananda, ed., *The Nectar of Chanting* (South Fallsburg, N.Y.: SYDA Foundation, 1975).

Swami Tapasyananda, trans., *Sri Vishnu Sahasranam* (Malapore, Madras: Sri Ramakrishna Math, 1986).

Howard J. Barrack, trans., *The Thousand Names of Vishnu* (New York: Tara Publications, 1974).

SAGES OF TAOISM

Tao Te Ching

All selections from Jonathan Star, trans., *Tao Te Ching,* (Princeton, N.J.: Theone Press, 1988).

Selections from verses 1, 25, 14, 47, 29, 50, 51, 76, 78, 22, 10.

Chuang Tzu

All selections rendered by Jonathan Star from Chapters 2, 4, 14, 19.

Sources:

Burton Watson, trans., *The Complete Works of Chuang Tzu* (New York: Columbia University Press, 1968).

Lionel Giles, trans., *Chuang Tzu* (London: Unwin Paperbacks, 1980).

Lin Yutang, trans., *The Wisdom of Lao Tzu* (New York: The Modern Library, 1948).

Lieh Tzu

Translated by Tzu-jan Wu.

BUDDHIST MASTERS

Eihei Dogen

All selections from Kazuaki Tanahashi, ed., *Moon in a Dewdrop: Writings of Zen Master Dogen* (San Francisco: North Point Press, 1985), 34–35.

Shakyamuni Buddha

All selections from P. Lal, trans., *The Dhammapada* (New York: Farrar, Straus and Giroux, 1967), 11, 18–20, 31.

The Dhammapada

All selections rendered by Jonathan Star.

Partial list of sources:

P. Lal, trans., *The Dhammapada* (New York: Farrar, Straus and Giroux, 1967).

Max Muller, trans., *The Dhammapada* (New York: Collier and Son, Sacred Books of the East, 1900).

Eknath Easwaran, trans., *The Dhammapada* (Petaluma, Calif.: Nilgiri Press, 1985).

B. Ananda Maitreya, trans., *The Dhammapada, the Path of Truth* (Novato, Calif.: Lotsawa, 1988).

Irving Babbitt, trans., *The Dhammapada* (New York: Oxford University Press, 1936).

Bassui Zenji

All selections from Philip Kapleau, *The Three Pillars of Zen* (Boston: Beacon Press, 1965), 160–161, 164, 169.

Huang Po

All selections from John Blofeld, trans., *The Zen Teachings of Huang Po* (New York: Grove Press, 1958), 29–30, 35–36, 131.

Shantideva

All selections from E. A. Burtt, trans., *Teachings of the Compassionate Buddha,* trans. L. D. Barnett (New York: New American Library, 1955), 135, 137.

Yung-chia

All selections from D. T. Suzuki, *Manual of Zen Buddhism* (New York: Grove Press, 1960), 97–100.

Gizan

Selected from W. Stryk and T. Ikemoto, *Zen Poems of China* (Garden City, N.Y.: Anchor Press/Doubleday, 1973), 69.

WISDOM OF THE HEBREWS

Book of Psalms

All selections rendered by Jonathan Star.

Wisdom of Solomon

All selections rendered by Jonathan Star.
Selections on pages 86 and 87 from Chapter 6.
Selection on pages 88–90 from Chapter 7.
Selection on page 91 from Chapter 8.

Ecclesiasticus

All sections from *The New English Bible* (New York: Oxford University Press, 1961).
Selection on pages 92–93 from Chapter 24, verses 1–6, 9–17.
Selection on page 94 from Chapter 1, verses 1–10 and Chapter 4, verses 11–13.

Selection on page 95 from Chapter 6, verses 36, 23–30.
Source consulted:
New American Standard Bible (Carol Stream, Ill.: Creation House, Inc., 1960).

STOIC PHILOSOPHERS

Marcus Aurelius

All selections rendered by Jonathan Star.
Selection on page 100 from Book 5:1 and 7:69.
Selection on page 101 from Book 2:4 and 2:17.
Selection on page 102 from Book 7:13, 11:9, and 6:44.
Selection on page 103 from Book 8:50.
Selection on page 104 from Book 5:6 and 4:3.
Selection on page 105 from Book 7:51, 7:68, and 7:57.
Selection on page 106 from Book 10:38, 5:21, and 7:59.
Selection on page 107 from Book 8:34, 4:23, and 10:16.

Partial list of sources:
Maxwell Staniforth, trans., *Marcus Aurelius: Meditations* (New York: Penguin Books, 1964).

G. H. Rendall, trans., *Marcus Aurelius Antoninus to Himself* (London: Macmillan and Co., 1898).

George Long, trans., *The Meditations of Marcus Aurelius* (New York: The Harvard Classics, P. F. Collier and Son, 1909).

C. R. Haines, trans., *Marcus Aurelius* (Cambridge, Mass.: Harvard University Press, 1916).

Epictetus

All selections adapted from Hastings Crossley, trans., *The Golden Sayings of Epictetus* (New York: P. F. Collier and Son, 1909), verses 77, 66, 1.

Seneca

All selections adapted from Chas Davis, *Greek and Roman Stoicism* (Boston: Herbert B. Turner and Co., 1903), 226, 241, 236.

SUFI POETS

Jalaluddin Rumi

All selections translated by Shahram Shiva and Jonathan Star from the *Diwan-i Shams-i Tabriz,* except "Come, come, whoever you are . . ." (page 118), which is traditional, and "All through time . . ." (page 125), which was rendered by Jonathan Star from R. H. Nicholson, *The Mystics of Islam* (New York: Shocken Books, 1975), 153.

Jami

Rendered by Jonathan Star from R. H. Nicholson, *The Mystics of Islam* (New York: Shocken Books, 1975), 81.

Ghalib

All selections rendered by Jonathan Star from Aijaz Ahmad, ed., *The Ghazals of Ghalib* (New York: Columbia University Press, 1971), ghazal 1, 4.

Nazir

Adapted by Jonathan Star from Bankey Behari, *Sufis, Mystics and Yogis of India* (Bombay: Bharatiya Vidya Bhavan, 1982), 183–188.

Fakhruddin Araqi

All selections translated by Shahram Shiva and Jonathan Star from *La'amat* (Divine flashes), flash 7, 14, 25, 27.

Ibn al Arabi

Adapted by Jonathan Star from Ralph Manheim, trans., *Creative Imagination in the Sufism of Ibn 'Arabi* (Princeton, N.J.: Princeton University Press, 1969), 174–175.

Mahmud Shabistari

All selections rendered by Jonathan Star.

Sources consulted:

E. H. Whinfield, trans., *The Secret Rose Garden* (London, 1880).

Florence Lederer, trans., *The Secret Rose Garden* (Grand Rapids, Mich.: Phanes Press, 1987).

Firdausi

Traditional translation.

CHRISTIAN SAINTS

Saint Paul

Selection on "Love" (pages 150–151) from I Corinthians 13:1–13. Rendered by Jonathan Star.

All other selections from *The New English Bible* (New York: Oxford University Press, 1961).

"The Apostles" (page 152) from I Corinthians 4:8–13 and II Corinthians 6:4–10.

"The Spirit" (page 153) from I Corinthians 12:4–11 and I Corinthians 3:16–17.

Philokalia

All selections from E. Kadloubovsky and G. E. H. Palmer, trans., *Early Fathers from the Philokalia* (London: Faber and Faber Limited, 1954), 109, 157–158, 161, 166, 170.

Selections on pages 154–155 are from St. Dorotheus.

First selection on page 156 is from Abba Evagrius.

Second and third selections on page 156 are from St. Nilus.

Meister Eckhart

All sections adapted by Jonathan Star from K. O. Schmidt, *Meister Eckhart's Way to Cosmic Consciousness,* trans. Léone Muller (Clayton, Georgia: Tri State Press, 1976), 128, 109; 70, 71; 124, 116, 63; 170, 80; 154, 161, 172.

Russian Monk

All selections from R. M. French, trans., *The Way of a Pilgrim* (New York: The Seabury Press, 1965), 1, 7, 31, 41, 105.

Thomas à Kempis

All selections from Richard Whitford, trans., *The Imitation of Christ,* adapted by Harold C. Gardiner (New York: Doubleday and Co., 1955), 109–111.

Jean Pierre de Caussade

All selections from John Beevers, trans., *Abandonment to Divine Providence* (New York: Doubleday, 1975), 25, 37, 40, 70, 73, 81–82; except "Come, all you simple souls . . ." (pages 166–167) and "There is nothing faith . . ." (page 170), which were adapted from Reverend H. Ramiere, trans., *Abandonment* (New York: Benziger Brothers, 1987), 79, 112; and "O Lord, let others . . ." (page 169), which was rendered by Jonathan Star.

POET-SAINTS OF INDIA

Shankaracharya

Selection on pages 179 and 180 are from Swami Prabhavananda and Christopher Isherwood, trans., *Shankara's Crest-Jewel of Discrimination* (Hollywood, California: Vedanta Press, 1947, 1975), 116, 121–123, 131–138.

Selection on page 181 is traditional.

Selection on pages 182–183 rendered by Jonathan Star from *The Six Stanzas of Salvation.*

Tukaram

Selections on pages 184 and 185 were adapted from John S. Hoyland, *An Indian Peasant Mystic* (Dublin, Ind.: Prinit Press, 1932), 43, 47; all other selections are from R. D. Ranade, *Mysticism in India* (Albany, N.Y.: SUNY Press, 1983), 303, 312, 320, 339, 349.

Jnaneshwar

Translated by Jonathan Star and Julle Lal from the *Amritanubhava*, Chapter 1; except the selections on pages 200 and 201, which are from B. P. Bahirat, *The Philosophy of Jnanadeva* (Bombay: Popular Book Depot, 1956), 150, 151; and the selection on page 229, which is from Swami Kripananda, *Jnaneshwar's Gita* (Albany, N.Y.: SUNY Press, 1989), 350.

Basavanna

All selections from A. K. Ramanujan, *Speaking of Shiva* (New York: Penguin Books, 1973), 83, 88.

Akkamahadevi

Selections on pages 204 and 205 from A. K. Ramanujan, *Speaking of Shiva* (New York: Penguin Books, 1973), 122, 139; except "It was like a flood . . ." (page 206), rendered by Julle Lal.

Mirabai

All selections rendered by Jonathan Star from Baldoon Dingra, trans., *Songs of Meera* (New Delhi: Vision Books, 1977), verse 4, 39, 78.

Ramdasa

All selections from R. D. Ranade, *Mysticism in India* (Albany, N.Y.: SUNY Press, 1983), 376–377, 391–392, 395, 410, 412–413, 415.

Swami Muktananda

All selections have been translated from Hindi to English by the editors and translators of SYDA Foundation.

Selection on "Perfect Beings" (page 218) is from Swami Muktananda, *Secret of the Siddhas* (South Fallsburg, N.Y.: SYDA Foundation, 1980), 57; and DARSHAN, 30/31:162 (1989).

Selection on "The Guru" (pages 219–220) is from Swami Muktananda, *I Have Become Alive* (South Fallsburg, N.Y.: SYDA Foundation, 1985), 29; and from an unpublished collection of talks.

Selection on "The World" (page 221) is from Swami Muktananda, *I Have Become Alive* (South Fallsburg, N.Y.: SYDA Foundation, 1985), 147/172, 203, 36/38.

Selection on "Love" (pages 222–223) is from Swami Muktananda, *I Have Become Alive* (South Fallsburg, N.Y.: SYDA Foundation, 1985), 175–177, 183.

Selection on "The Universal Energy" (page 224) is from Swami Muktananda, *Siddha Meditation* (South Fallsburg, N.Y.: SYDA Foundation, 1977), 60.

Selection on "Play of Consciousness" (page 225) is from Swami Muktananda, *Play of Consciousness* (South Fallsburg, N.Y.: SYDA Foundation, 1978), 183.

Selection on "The Kingdom Within" (pages 226–228) is from an unpublished collection of talks.

CREDITS